Surviving
Has Made Me
Crazy

Surviving Has Made Me Crazy

POEMS

Mark Nepo

CavanKerry ❖ Press LTD.

Library of Congress Cataloging-in-Publication Data

Nepo, Mark.
Surviving has made me crazy : poems / Mark Nepo. — 1st ed.
p. cm.
ISBN-13: 978-1-933880-01-3
ISBN-10: 1-933880-01-5
1. Lymphoma—Patients—Poetry. I. Title.

PS3564.E6S87 2007
811'.54—dc22

2006036860

Author photograph by Don McIlraith © 2006
Cover art: "Surviving Has Made Me Crazy" by Peter Cusack © 2006
Cover and book design by Peter Cusack

CavanKerry Press Ltd.
Fort Lee, New Jersey
www.cavankerrypress.org

First Edition 2007
Printed in the United States of America

LaurelBooks

Surviving Has Made Me Crazy is the fourth title of CavanKerry's Literature of Illness imprint. LaurelBooks are fine collections of poetry and prose that explore the many poignant issues associated with confronting serious physical and/or psychological illness.

CavanKerry is grateful to the Arnold P. Gold Foundation for the Advancement of Humanism in Medicine for joining us in sponsoring this imprint. Offering LaurelBooks as teaching tools to medical schools is the result of shared concerns—humanism, community, and meeting the needs of the underserved. Together with the Gold Foundation, CavanKerry's two outreach efforts, *GiftBooks* and *Presenting Poetry & Prose*, bring complimentary books and readings to the medical community at major hospitals across the United States.

The Arnold P. Gold Foundation

CavanKerry Press is grateful for the support it
receives from the New Jersey State Council on the Arts.

Acknowledgments

Thanks for permission to excerpt from the following previously published works:

"Surviving Has Made Me Crazy" is kindly reprinted from *Acre of Light* (Greenfield Review Press, 1994) and *Suite for the Living* (Bread for the Journey, 2004).

"Opening Without Words" first appeared in *Sabbath: Restoring the Sacred Rhythm of Rest*, Wayne Muller (Bantam, 1999).

Epigraph for section 1 is reprinted with permission, from "The Survivors" in *Collected Poems 1945–1990*, R. S. Thomas. Copyright © 2002, published by Phoenix Press, a division of The Orion Publishing Group.

UPON SEEKING TU FU AS A GUIDE

And so I asked him, how is it God is everywhere and nowhere? He circled me like a self I couldn't reach, "Because humans refuse to live their lives." I was confused. He continued, "You hover rather than enter." I was still confused. He spoke in my ear, "God is only visible within your moment entered like a burning lake." I grew frightened. He laughed, "Even now, you peer at me as if what you see and hear are not a part of you." I grew angry. He ignored me, "You peer at the edge of your life, so frantic to know, so unwilling to believe." Indeed, I was frantic. He was in my face, "And now that you have cancer, you ask to be spared." I grew depressed. He took my shoulders, "For God's sake! Enter your own life! Enter!"

Table of Contents

Foreword xv
About the Journey xxi

THROUGH THE CRACKS

Thoracic Surgery 3
Today I Feel the Pain of the World 5
Eyeless Beauty 7
The Mistake 8
Secretions 9
Nothing As It Was 10
The Flute of Interior Time 13
The Thing About Darkness 14
Sweating Between Worlds 15
Living Through Things 16
The Bells, Not the Church 17
All the While 19
Only Singers in the Temple 20
Upon the Death of a Friend 22
In the Other Kind of Time 23
Belief in the Invisible 24
You'll Get Over It 26

LEAD AND DRAG

Before the Rain 31
Water of Greenness 32
The Edge 33
White Tea 35

Basements and Dreams 37

The Friend 39

More Dreams 41

Requiem for a Father Missing 42

For Three Voices Lost in Flight 47

Opening Without Words 48

Peril 49

Inch of Karma 51

Note on the Fridge for You 53

On One Corner 54

Ladders to Nowhere 55

Talkin' About Everything 56

The Salt of Our History 58

WEAK ENOUGH

Diapedesis 61

Strange and Beautiful 63

How to Mourn a Miracle 64

While I Was There 65

For the One Who Misses Laughter 69

A Vow Beyond Awareness 70

Hearing Good Advice 71

Five Thousand Ways to Listen 72

The Crows Between Us 74

Fires Looking for a Sea 76

Earth Guest 78

For the Circle 80

Howard is My Brother 81

Mother and Child 84

Burning the Wrapper 85

The Mystery of Illness 87

Carried Home 88

God's Timing 89

CROSSING OVER

The Leaving 93
For Crying Outloud 94
More Mysterious Than Regret 95
Lesson from the Farther Shore 97
You're Looking Great 99
How I Loved Them 100
The Dream of Healing 103
Made Less and More 104
Released 106
The Ache of Being Alive 107
Dropping Below 108
As Moonlight 110
Nothing Has Grown Over 112
Four Dreams of Death 114
Surviving Has Made Me Crazy 118

Gratitudes 119

Foreword

Close on the heels of my own father's passing, just ten days ago, I must admit that my tears at having read Mark's words are hardly dry as I write these. It would be simple, and true, to say that Mark has a unique ability to write from the heart, revealing deep emotional and intellectual truths. But any attempt I might make to point to these truths would necessarily fall short of the truths themselves and the way they are told. Since I am a scientist and not a poet, I will have to rely on a different method for introducing this volume to you.

I was raised in a family of scientists who always asked, "What's the evidence?" It didn't really matter what the topic was, the question of evidence was always the same. Like Cuba Gooding's character in the film *Jerry Maguire* who challenges Tom Cruise to "Show me the money!", I have always been an empiricist relying on the evidence of things seen to guide decision making in my life. So it was with some consternation that I found my eyes rimming with tears as I read "The Edge," a poem and parable about the ultimate incomprehensibility of life. Scientist or not, there was something in the poem that moved me deeply, connected me to my recent experience of loss, something in my response which I could not explain on the basis of empirical evidence. I was left with a residue of strong emotion but no way to explain where it had come from or why. The small but important transformation I experienced in reading Mark's poem is emblematic of similar changes that are occurring in medical research and clinical care. Changes that make Mark's work all the more important and relevant.

At the core of modern medicine's understanding of disease is a concept known as "homeostasis." The term, coined in 1932 by Walter Cannon, a Harvard physiologist, literally means "resistance to change" (from the Greek *homoios*, meaning "the same, like, resembling"; and *stasis*, meaning "to stand"). This core understanding holds that ecological, biological, and social systems are homeostatic. They oppose change in every conceivable way in order to remain in a steady state. These systems exhibit the remarkable property of reacting to disturbances in their environment by creating equal and opposite modifications. The goal of these modifications is to resist change and maintain the status quo. In the truest sense of the word, these systems are conservative.

It is relatively easy to see how the concept of homeostasis comes into play in clinical medicine. Physicians are taught to view disease as pathological disturbances of biological systems. If left unchecked, these disturbances can lead to the destruction of the system. Cancer is good example of a physiological system in dis-equilibrium. Uncontrolled cell growth threatens to destroy normal tissue and organs leading, if left untreated, to the death of the individual. The goal of treatment is to halt pathological cell growth and return the body to its previous state of equilibrium. Cure in medicine is, literally, conservation of the body. This physiological view of disease and treatment has stood the test of time and has led to marvelous progress in treating diseases that once meant swift and certain death. Indeed, the primary cause of pre-mature death at the beginning of the twentieth century was disease; today, it is accidents and environmental events.

While continuing to answer questions such as "What causes cancer?" or "Why does the body age?" scientific inquiry has turned to new questions about the dynamic and sometimes unpredictable influences of psychological and social functioning on physiological processes. In the brave new world of integrated scientific thinking, it is possible now to ask questions like, "How does a poem, work of art, or empathic gesture influence the experience of a person living with a life-threatening disease and those around her, including her physician?" or "What effect does writing about the emotional experience of disease have on physiological functioning?" A recent study in the *Journal of the American Medical Association* showed that patients with rheumatoid arthritis or asthma who wrote for twenty minutes a day about their emotions received the same physiological benefit as the standard medical treatment of inhaled or ingested steroids!

It was Descartes, the eighteenth-century philosopher, who put forward a theory that separated mind and body, a notion that found favor in scientific circles for well over two hundred years. Proponents of this view can still be found today, but the preponderance of evidence is that thoughts, feelings, and biochemical activity all relate to one another at some level. In addition to being organisms whose biological equilibrium is dis-eased, we are mothers, fathers, children, friends, and lovers who experience strong social and emotional responses to disease. In other words, we experience psychological, social, and symbolic realities in addition to whatever is happening physiologically. George Engel, a physician and father of the biopsychosocial model of medicine, draws a useful distinction here between disease, defined as a biological state, and illness, defined as a person's social and psychological response to disease.

During the last forty years, researchers in the biopsychosocial tradition have documented various ways in which thinking and feeling relate to biological functioning from the sub-cellular to the socio-cultural level. In actuality, the realities of mind and body are not separate, as Descartes claimed, but are, rather, part of the same living systems that include experience and affect. One important consequence of this insight is that it adds a new dimension to the concept of cure. This new dimension of healing is understood as the myriad ways in which human beings make sense out of being in a state of dis-ease.

Herein lies the key to Mark's genius as a poet and philosopher. He asserts, and I believe rightly so, that the experience of surviving a life threatening disease is not a return to homeostasis, the way things were, but rather a radical transformation from which there is no turning back. As he writes in "Thoracic Surgery," "I've had to redefine normal like putting grit in paint." Once you've added a new ingredient to the mix you have something that cannot be transformed back to the way it was. Like Gregor Samsa, the character in Franz Kafka's short story *Metamorphosis*, who discovers that he's been transformed into a cockroach in a world that does not recognize the change—it's enough to make anyone crazy.

Many of the poems in this book explore the landscape of inner experience that is transformed by illness. In this territory, mundane experiences of everyday life that might go unnoticed or be taken for granted have powerful lessons to teach. In "Note on the Fridge for You," for example, Mark asserts, "I have no particular wisdom about this. Just that almost dying has carved me a third eye that sometimes sees, but which often waters until I see nothing. I know death is with me often, nearby, over my shoulder, and the trick, if there is one, is to feel its insistence on how precious everything is without turning around too much, getting caught in its stare. It has made me look for eternity inside your eyes, in the silence of the willow, in our dog's sleepy breathing—rather than in the field of unlived years."

Similarly, the paradox of living in an everyday world and simultaneously being connected to something larger appears in many of these poems. "Belief in the Invisible," a poem about spiritual awareness, reflects this theme. Consider the wisdom in Mark's statement that "Half of what I write is because I've left the door open for the invisible. The other half comes from living in the world." He continues, "And leaving something out for an invisible guest has become a lifelong practice by which I bow to the mysteries hoping they will show themselves, like leaving bread for ducks to appear so we might see them take off in their splendor, so much more colorful with their wings unfurled." Surely, one cannot read these lines, even in the harsh light of scientific rhetoric, without being moved.

Another compelling theme addressed in this volume is the question of intimacy. Why, for example, do we wait until someone dies or moves away to share our "true" feelings of love and respect? Mark's response to this question is straightforward. The benefits of showing up fully at every moment are worth the risk of fear, embarrassment, and superficiality that attend relationships built on convenience or the status quo. In "Fires Looking for a Sea," Mark reflects, "All my life I've tried to lessen what stands between my heart and the world, between my mind and the sky, between my eye and your eye."

Reflecting on the themes in this book, I think I have a better idea of why I am so moved by its content. It's because Mark embodies what we all strive for in life—authenticity, a discerning eye and clear voice, and the ability to bear witness to the pain and pleasure of living without retreating into sentimentality or solipsism. In real terms, these poems are medicine. They have offered me the gift of companionship and guidance as I sort through the meaning of my own loss, my own resistance to change, and the transformations of self and spirit that await if I am open to them. Surviving cancer may have made the author crazy but it has also given us the gift of a truly gracious and generous mind and heart.

— Rich Frankel Ph.D.
Professor of Medicine and Geriatrics
Senior Research Scientist,
Regenstrief Institute
Indiana University School of Medicine
November 2006

About the Journey

It has been eighteen years since I was first diagnosed with cancer and I have never been the same. In some ways, I am still stunned to be here. And but for a hiccup of God, I could be dead and one of those I've loved and lost along the way might be writing this to you. So this is not a book on how to get past illness. I've never gotten past it. Rather, it has turned me inside out. More humbly, this is a blanket of twigs and berries gathered on my way through the long forest. They are the few things that haven't gone bad. And no matter how little there seems to be, I now know, it is enough. There is plenty for everyone. If the twigs can light a fire and the berries feed you, something will have passed between us.

But I'm getting ahead of myself. Before I had cancer, I had many ambitions. I was teaching and desperately wanting to get published, seeking affirmation everywhere, when I was tripped up. Ann was my partner at the time. In all, we were together for twenty years. But after helping to save each other's lives, the stone of that event rippled us in different directions and we are no longer together.

To share the story of my own transformation, we must go back to 1987, when, after nine years of marriage, Ann and I were both stricken with cancer. The months became a labyrinth. In May, Ann was diagnosed as having cervical in situ. This led to her having a conization in June and a hysterectomy that August. At the same time, I had a mysterious lump forming on my head, which turned out to be growing underneath the skull as well. It grew to the size of half a grapefruit. And so, mere days after her surgery, I entered the hospital, moving through a gauntlet of tests, including a biopsy which diagnosed this strange lesion as a lymphoma lodged between my brain and skull. It was eating through the bone. Finally, after much desperation and prayer and visualization and fighting with and against doctors, the tumor, both below the skull and above, vanished, avoiding major brain surgery, whole head radiation, and spinal chemotherapy.

The doctors could not explain it and our friends and family helped us limp back to life, a struggle in itself, which we were shaping strongly until November of '88 when a spot on my eighth rib began to grow. We were crushed. By January, a lump filled Ann's palm as we hugged. In February of '89, I underwent thoracic surgery to remove that rib and its adjacent muscles. The cells in that rib were clearly malignant and so, barely repaired, I embarked on four months of chemotherapy. Today, as of our last checkup, we are both well, and forever changed.

In truth, this experience has unraveled the way I see the world. It has scoured my lens of perception, landing me in a deeper sense of living. Both Ann and I were, against our will, reduced, with our mouths open, into the mystery of life in which we all swim and from which we all emerge on our separate shores. And spit up, naked and exhausted, it's clear that, being human, we are each a crucible, an ever-changing inlet through which the greater Whole in all its forms ebbs and flows.

I have, quite frankly, found death at my shoulder earlier than most. Yet I have also been touched by a relentless, mysterious grace which surfaced briefly to restore me. Now I find myself tied to a fathomless place where I had not dared to voyage. I call that reservoir God, though you may call it something else.

Now, all these years later, I find myself devoted to eternity opened by the moment. This stems from the fact that I have been broken by disease and know, beyond any doubt, that there are moments endured from which our lives will never be the same; severe moments beyond which everything is changed. No one asks for these moments. They simply happen the way a merciless wind cracks a tree we never imagined would crack. But it is the wind of all time breathing through our cracks that transforms us.

A few days after the World Trade Center came down, I was co-leading a retreat in New Hampshire for cancer patients, their loved ones, survivors, and healing professionals. The events of the week were heavily present in the room, when a bandaged woman in a wheelchair spoke. She had just gone through her third surgery to remove metastasized tumors. She wet her dry, swollen lips and said, "It's a terrible thing . . . but now we all belong to the same club." There was a huge sigh from everyone in the room. As a survivor, I understood what she was saying: that the fragility of life was now uppermost in people's minds, that fear and uncertainty made every moment precious, that the illusion that we are immune to being changed was shattered. In ordinary time, people sail through their lives under the misconception that loss and transformation happen to other people. But once experience leads us beneath that illusion, we find ourselves as rare as seeds on the wind, and anything that grows us is a blessing to be prayed for.

A word about this book, which has been ripening for a long time. Ever since I awoke from my surgeries, I have been learning how integrated and useful everything is. And so, this book is not separated into cancer poems and living poems. It is not arranged chronologically, but more as a mix of then and now, as they are never far from each other: the wound and the healing, the fear and the peace, the confusion and the clarity.

In essence, if blessed, some event or lack of event undoes us until we are broken open into honest living. For me, that event was cancer. But it could be anything, at any time. What opens us may differ, but what it is that opens and what such parting can do to us is the same. So, while this all starts with illness and refers back to its canyon and its precipice, the lessons that have come through and reshaped me with their scouring belong to everyone.

This is what I have to offer. You see, the handles to all my cups have been broken off, so that I might learn that to touch and to drink are the same thing. These poems are such handle-less cups.

— MN

Through the Cracks

Friend, I say,
since we are at death's
door, come in,
let us peer at eternity
through the cracks
in each other's hearts.

— R. S. Thomas

THORACIC SURGERY

It was like jumping
with full consent
into an empty well
so deep I only remember
falling in the dark
till falling without
direction put me to sleep.
Then I woke broken
and battered with no
memory of impact.
Ever since, it's been
impossible to let go
and I tire and ache.
When I do sleep, I
wake with this shoulder
burning or that flank of
muscle bound or the veter-
brae in my neck locked. Afraid
to let go. Never knowing how
or if I'll wake. And true,
the trauma and pain echo
smaller and smaller. But
I've had to redefine
normal like putting
grit in paint. For
to breathe is sore;
to inhale, in-sore;
to exhale, out-sore;
to dream, bright
and sore. And now
after 12 injections

of morphine and
180 capsules of
codeine, I fear
the unanesthetized
days. Now I'm told
a side effect is
depression—the heart
grown sore. Now I must
strip the medicine
like clothes. The
depression, like
a zippered cloud
around my head.
Must nakedly
with full consent
jump back
into the world.
Everyone's saying—
C'mon. Let's go.
But I entered this
and nothing's been
the same. How can I
jump on out and not
fear the world is
a broken cage?

TODAY I FEEL THE PAIN OF THE WORLD

My dog's hips grind where no one can see.
She wants to keep up, but has to sit.
I take her home, pet her a while,
and go for groceries where
the old man packing bags
is staring off. I know by his heavy
silver eyes that he is a widower
and just as he lifts my no-fat cottage cheese
he sees her floating somewhere before him
and the soda and the swordfish and the English
muffins are piling up as the black belt keeps
moving, and I gently take the cottage cheese
from his hand, and he returns, looking at
me, a bit dizzy to still be here.
He sighs, rubs his eye, and asks, "Paper
or plastic?" I help him bag
what no one can bag.

After putting soda in the fridge
I eat out anyway, and next to me,
a small woman trying to be heard
while her large partner pretends nothing
is wrong. She knocks over the salt as he
butters his bread. He shakes his head
and wonders who she is.

Beyond them, in a booth by a window,
an elderly couple. It is clear they can't speak.
They sign each other and their faces
are lively with yes and no and in between.
Suddenly over coffee, the man sees something

across the road. He's full of joy, pointing
and smiling, wanting his wife to see.
It could be a hawk opening its wings
or a burst of light budding
a thin maple.

His wife never really sees
but he thinks she does
and he feels relieved.

I realize we are all this way.
Whether seeing dead faces at the register
or butterflies behind light poles, sometimes
the skin of mind is torn and we are not
separate beings. Once the talking is done,
we point and point at the proofs of love
for all we're worth.

I feel more today
than one being should
and can't tell
if I'm in trouble
or on holy ground.

EYELESS BEAUTY

Each of us,
especially the newborn,
with a piece of knowing
no one else has.

Each born with
a double hunger:
for the peace within
and its conflict without.

Near-death can switch the hungers.

I am between hungers,
still as a branch
on which
a mute red bird
is about to land.

THE MISTAKE

The wind had been knocked out of me
and doubled over, I looked like I was asking
for something. It was then that someone
passing by offered me something precious,
which I managed to hold briefly before
dropping. And when I dropped it,
it fell into someone else's hands
and she was so grateful.
She called me kind and generous.
She couldn't thank me enough.
But it was only a mistake.
I felt compelled to admit
that I had merely dropped
something precious. At this,
she put what I had dropped down
and took my face and said, "Don't
you see? Even dropping what is precious
is a gift." It made me cry and while
she rocked me, what was precious
rolled toward a bird who fluttered
over it. It finally landed at the feet
of a small child who hugged what was
given, what was dropped, what was a
mistake, what was let go in order to hold
someone lost. The little one just hugged it
and turned to her mother in awe, shouting,
"Look what I found! Look what I found!"

SECRETIONS

Why not have the truth?

Why not ask the soft one
born with sad eyes
about unending sadness?

Who is it we protect
with our secrets?

What God is served
if I am not told
how long I have to live?

And who presumes to know?
Whose little cave is that?

And what if I refuse it all,
the pronouncement of death,
the whispers,
the implacable smiles?

What if I just eat the truth—
like a refugee nibbling wild berries—
and live?

NOTHING AS IT WAS

1. EVER DOWN
(APRIL 1983)

Why is it I can remember nothing as it was? Nothing. Just that kitchen table where we rearranged each other's faces like condemned chancellors; never allowed to forget our capacity for failure. That table, Mother, where we passed the red wine, while you drew the world tighter, twisting out advice that justified your poor choices. You've always been telling us what you wanted. And Dad was weak, afraid to venture from your magnetic bed. Why so much anger in our home? Why so many shadows? My brother's neck bulged at your prodding. You called it teasing. But when I was in South Africa, I saw Afrikaner boys poking a hungry dog with a stick in much the same way. It was at that table that you told us how handicapped you were for bringing us into the world—twice pregnant with nowhere to go—poked by the fates. We've always argued and fallen and never cracked, clenching our teeth to bring home a point. We have had too much sharpness and too many points. You recognize that clench of teeth as yours. Why so much poison around that table, even in the center which I thought sacred?

When we went to college, I kept dreaming of withstanding you. Now, I polish the table in my own house, eager for failed chancellors to dine with. Still, I dream of melting you back to your hot beginning before this muteness set in, before you became transfixed with hammering your dark spikes into the world—pinning things, critiquing things, dismantling things that could have bloomed. How do we share our futures when they threaten your past?

Why do you keep mailing us maps of the ruin? We sleep with them and you and wake all confused. We travel long gray highways to hug your face, to kiss your mouth, to suck at your secret like a cold breast. All the while, you rim the table with your dark monologue. We eat your love and go groggy, and you say, staring into your very strong coffee, "Dreams die hard."

2. BAD NEEDLES
(JUNE 1999)

I was on an examination table with an IV needle in my left arm. It was nothing serious, but Susan was concerned. Some test was being done. Someone was next to me, also having blood drawn. The nurse was busy with this other person. The needle in my arm was sore and my bicep was beginning to swell. Susan noticed the swelling and said, "Something's wrong. Why don't you tell the nurse?" I said, "No. It's nothing serious. They just didn't do a good job of putting the needle in. It's alright." The nurse, without looking up, jiggled the tube collecting my blood, while treating the other patient. I said, "Thank you." She said, again without looking up, half-sarcastically, and half in admiration, "We treat him like hell and he thanks us." Part of me took it as a compliment. But Susan was furious.

Now I realize that, for much of my life, I have accepted bad needles and said it is alright. I'm almost polite, accepting ill treatment in order to be seen as good and kind. I feel, all too often, that if I say the needle has been put in badly, I'm causing trouble or being ungrateful or complaining. Worse, there have been times I've pretended that there isn't even a needle stuck in me, so as not to hurt the one poking. For the first time, I see how I've colluded in my suffering. Like a fish who dreams the hook will save him.

3. ON THE DEATH OF MY MOTHER IN A DREAM
(JUNE 2005)

It was the slowest fall I've ever seen. It took longer than my life. She was sneaking a cigarette with her black cup of coffee when her mouth fell open like a fish. And as she fell, so fell my evidence. Now it was safe to look more closely at her face. Under the angry mask, she was frightened. She'd held onto a dark rope all her life, twisting and tightening. But mostly, she was frightened. Now I could finally weep for her. God, I came from this stranger and, by being who I am, I've somehow completed something she meant to start. Somehow, in reaching what she couldn't, the cost has been not being loved by her. She laid there, like a dark fish too far away from water, her small mouth open, all the things she never said rising like smoke. Her unfinished cigarette kept burning. Her death will be sad and liberating. I fear it will come like a smolder of peace when the fire that has raged across my life, the fire that I came from, will finally go out.

4. NO MORE AMBITIONS
(NOVEMBER 2005)

Oddly, beautifully, I have no more ambitions, not even to write a book. The expressions are more a form of inner breathing . . . We don't weave tapestries of the air, we only breathe and live . . . The sun doesn't build with its light, yet everything lighted grows . . . This is new and I am strangely not content, but disoriented as the maturation of my self has eliminated what I thought was my self. The few kind enough to listen are happy for me. They say I'm on holy ground. But though I feel on the edge of joy, I am not doused in joy. Though I feel on the edge of breaking, some pit at center has not broken. I know, way down, the two are related. To know joy we must break, for only the deepest part exposed can feel completely alive. In fact, I think this is joy—the sensation of air hitting the softest, deepest place again and again as if for the first time . . . Now that I know the sensation of deep love, I cannot imagine what to do with it, other than to love.

THE FLUTE OF INTERIOR TIME

If you are never hungry,
how can you know
the contours of your stomach.

If you are never thirsty,
how can you know
the edges of your voice.

If you are never disappointed,
how can you know
the reaches of your heart.

If you are never in doubt,
how can you know
the ceiling of your mind.

If you are never empty,
how can you know
the fullness of your spirit.

If you are never alone,
how can you know
God.

THE THING ABOUT DARKNESS

When I am closest to the earth,
often after a fall, I somehow know
that the side of God's face that goes dark
does so the way the moon goes dark
because we, like the earth, turn away.

It's how most things go dark. Not because
they are dark, but because we can't or won't
turn with them as they follow the light.

It is we who seldom own the distance we
create. It is this distance that often creates
darkness. And evil arises when those who
resist the inevitable pull into life make
an enemy of all that they have
distanced themselves from.

SWEATING BETWEEN WORLDS

I never told you but sweating on morphine after having my rib removed I
dreamt of you . . .

The house we lived in is dark. No one seems to be up. The water in the
kitchen sink is beginning to overflow. The faucets in the wall no longer
work. I am ten or eleven, and, like Hans Brinker, I try to put my fingers in
the sea wall, though I secretly want it to flow, to flood the house. I love the
clear water and feel safe in its presence. But I know I am supposed to dam
it up. That it is flowing and that the faucets are broken is a mistake. My
small fingers aren't enough to stop the flow. It is then I see you at a desk in
the corner. Your back is to me. You seem to be in a very quiet conversation
on the phone. I leave the sink and ask you to fix the pipes. As I approach, I
hear you say into the phone, "Mark is up. I can't talk right now." I feel
excluded, but it feels familiar. I wonder who you can be talking to and what
you could be saying that I shouldn't hear. I ask you, "Daddy, please, fix the
pipes," but you never even look at me. You just keep staring into the desk,
the phone in your ear. You don't hang up and it's clear that, as soon as I
leave, you will continue your conversation. You usher me off, "You can fix
it yourself. Go ahead." I go back to the sink and watch the water flow and
flow. You lean into the phone and resume your secret conversation. You
never look at me again. I really don't want to fix the pipes. I want to let it
all flood the house, drowning everyone but me. I watch the water overflow
the basin, not knowing what to do . . .

That day, I realized how much it has taken to uphold you both, to maintain
the possibility in my mind of your goodness. Today, I realize I have toiled
like some sort of closet-Atlas, straining to keep what I need from you before
me. And having a rib ripped from me, I've let you slip and drop, at first
feeling weak for letting you down. But the truth is that none of us are in
Eden and you have landed into just who you are.

LIVING THROUGH THINGS

When wiggling through a hole
the world looks different than
when scrubbed clean by the wiggle
and looking back.

THE BELLS, NOT THE CHURCH

They had been digging in with each other
and seemed tangled in the weeds of failed
relationships. So there was a certain distance
between them as they were driving home on
Sunday morning, when a deer, startled into
the road, crumpled their windshield, red fur
and pellets of glass across their faces. They
each had small cuts which the other had to
tend and a certain gentleness was born.

My wife before bed in the dark said quietly,
"Perhaps that deer was called to pass its
gentleness through that windshield, right
into their trembling hearts." Who can say
the Universe doesn't work this way?

A few days later, she tells me of a town
in New England whose church bells rang
for generations, but when the church was
taken down, the farmers missed the bells,
not the church.

I watch her when she sleeps and how our
dog just waits for her to wake. I watch when
she reaches to fill the bird feeder. She talks
to them and the finch, especially, seems
to listen.

I wonder what the birds and animals say
to her. But watching, I know. It is the bells,
not the church. The gentleness, not what is

broken between us. It is the things Susan sees,
not my want to know them.

Tonight, we will go to a gallery where clay
she has shaped and fired in the earth will
rest in the wordless open, and I, along with
others, will want to touch what has been
fired, though the signs say not to.

ALL THE WHILE

The moon begins by humming low.
It turns the forest branches blue and
makes the smaller animals lift their furry
heads, their marble eyes reflecting
soft slivers of moonlight.

Like constellations on earth not yet
in place. Like paradigms of truth that
keep moving after you name them.

And so the Universe tunes itself,
one living thing finding its pitch
by the sound and light of another.

It tells me that somewhere
in the country of blue silence,
the groans give off soft flares of light
by which we navigate our suffering.

So despite what others say, there is
a web-like blueprint that breathes.
Made invisible by our despair and
disbelief. Made to seem so far away
each time we drink from the illusion
that we are alone.

And all the while, the moon—
like the ageless dream that outlives
all dreamers—begins
by humming low.

ONLY SINGERS IN THE TEMPLE

O Eden is where the light
is strong and nothing
covers your eyes.

I am 55, have lived many lives, have survived cancer and a cold mother, have tried to hold onto friends like food for thirty years, and I confess that I have often been my own undoing.

To be honest, I have awakened and closed for more than half a century—have run from and to, have climbed and fallen down, have lifted and broken many precious things. And still, I cry out for love when alone and cry out for space when loved. Still, I ask questions that can never be answered and live like a premise to all that is never asked. I keep moving what should be left alone and dropping what can't be carried.

Over the years, I have been broken of my stubbornness into accepting a great many things. Though I started out trying to fill my loneliness by chasing after others, I had to accept that no one could find the roots in that dark hole but me. Though I started out determined to achieve greatness as a poet, like Icarus, the closer I got to the Source, the more it melted me back into my humanness. And though, during my days of cancer, I wanted to be spared from my suffering, I was humbled to lay flat on the earth where I finally heard the fire at the center. I can only admit that, starting out with dreams of being a great conductor, I landed as a thorough note in hopes of being sung. And I am happier for it.

Now, on the other side, it's harder to pretend, less and less wiggle room. Now that skin and air meet, I wonder how anything can last. Yet once everything is out of the way, once I am out of the way, there is no lasting or not lasting, only the rub of what is human against the Divine. The medicine is in showing the human workings along the way and how suffering redresses our lens. Though it seems obvious, suffering is just a slow form of revelation, the inevitable remover of all that films the heart.

You see, I've aspired to great things only to beg for another day, have been tenacious to the point of surrender. And now it is about climbing into the open until opening is climbing, not going beyond the living, not disappearing into ideas of piety or air. But rooting like a vein or artery entangled in the mess of muscle and flesh and blood that somehow lifts a cup to the lip.

When I go inside far enough, I can feel my grandmother's warm breath wash over me as she turned from baking in her little brick apartment. I can feel the sweat from her lip on my boyish head. Or the moment of waking after surgery sooner than they had planned, feeling my bones like white twigs pulsing. I guess I've always been awake sooner than expected, was even born a month too soon. It's how I know that piano music and waves come from the same place.

UPON THE DEATH OF A FRIEND
(FOR WINK)

I have given up trying to be strong.
I have given up trying to understand.
I only know that you are not here.
I see your smile. I hear your laugh.
But you are now part of the air
I breathe after crying that
you are gone.

There were others closer to you.
Others who knew you longer.
But you never gave up your
covenant with life. For this,
I loved you.

After the service, I didn't
want to leave. I didn't want
the post-you world to begin.

But the candle went out
and someone needed to go
to the bathroom, and the day
had to end. And you began
your life after life as the silence
that makes those who knew you
dream of birds and lakes
reflecting their song.

IN THE OTHER KIND OF TIME

Let's journey now
to the other kind of time
where we've known each other
for centuries, beneath our names,
beneath our pain, to the other side
where we can stop to listen
the way fox listen to the night.

Come with me out of the cold
where we can put down the
notions we've been carrying
like torn flags into battle.

We can throw them to the earth
or place them in the earth, and ask,
why these patterns in the first place?
If you want, we can repair them, if
they still seem true. Or we can
sing as they burn.

Come. Let's feel our way
beneath the noise where we
can ask what it means to be alive
and lift our chins from the stream
like deer who've outrun
all the hunters.

BELIEF IN THE INVISIBLE

It was a small moment during Passover when I was a boy. We'd drive to Baldwin where my mother's parents lived. Pop was a furrier from Rumania. He had a great laugh which opened his entire face and I was always drawn to peer through to a mysterious plateau where life had led him. He'd had his hardships: fleeing persecution in Europe as a boy, leaving his family, losing his brothers, crossing the cold Atlantic. And yet, he'd landed through endless gratitude somewhere on God's invisible mountain where the air alone made him laugh.

Well, we'd drive the twenty minutes down Sunrise Highway to see them on Passover. And though we'd read the Haggadah and mouth the ancient blessings, recounting how God passed over the first born in another time, another place, it was the glass of wine left in the middle of the table for Elijah that taught me about faith. As done for centuries, the front door was left ajar, the filled glass set on the table as a quiet offering to the prophet-angel. And leaving the door open all night strangely made the world seem safer, bigger.

It made me realize at an early age that there is more power in inviting things in than keeping things out. And leaving something out for an invisible guest has become a lifelong practice by which I bow to the mysteries hoping they will show themselves. Like leaving bread for ducks to appear so we might see them take off in their splendor, much more colorful with their wings unfurled. Half of what I write is because I've left the door open for the invisible. The other half comes from living in the world. You see, Pop taught me that, no matter how little you have on your table, it's just as important to leave something for the invisible stranger as to save or give.

So, Pop would play with us after dinner, chasing us from room to room. And suddenly, miraculously, he'd stop as we'd circle the cleaned up table, and with astonishment, he'd point to the half-empty glass and gasp, "Look!

Elijah Was Here!" We were always dumb founded. We'd get real close to the glass, to be sure the wine had actually been drunk. Then, we'd race to the open door and look up and down the night-lit street. Once, I ran down the stoop, to the end of the block, and I swear I could almost feel the whip of Elijah's robe.

In a few years, my mother, thinking she was doing us a favor, let us know that Pop would somehow slip away and drink the wine. She said this not in malice, but as if she were arming us against a cruel world. But even knowing this did not undermine my belief in the unseen. For more than all of it—more than Pop's loving effort to have us believe and my mother's loving effort to have us see through it—more than this, I'm grateful to Pop for teaching me to always leave the door open. That while there are things to be afraid of, there is more to be thankful for.

YOU'LL GET OVER IT

No one prepared me
for the lightning swing of mood
or the courage turned sober
like a stack of dirty plates.

Now when someone dies
of what I had, I fistup
like a clam, spindrift
through the deep, and
shudder at how much
time there is.

When it blackens
my inner eye,
some brief secret
like a brother's child
says my name
and I start to weep.

This aftermath is more
than stitches disappearing
in the scalp.

On good days
the bare thrill of being
surpasses any drug.

On bad days, well
today is good
and though I mourn
the scattering of spores

that do not become a tree
and the jellied mass of eggs
beneath the mother fish
that are eaten or crushed,
I rise, a lone surviving dot
that sprouts into its dream.

Lead and Drag

The fates lead those who will,
those who won't they drag.

— an old Roman saying

BEFORE THE RAIN

I dreamt of Michael,
that son of a bitch,
always glaring.

I went behind
and found him kneeling
in his wound.

He said, "I can't do this anymore."
I knelt beside him, "No one needs you to."
"But" he said and started to retreat.

I helped him to his feet and standing up,
his wound didn't seem so big, and beyond
its rim, there were skies and oceans
and new music and laughter.

Standing this way together
in awe of the sky,
it was how we met.

His eyes softened
and I remembered
how much I love him.

WATER OF GREENNESS

Oddly, on the next page,
a photo of a Chinese junk on
the Canton River, whose rail is close
to being submerged, and all at once,
I am twelve, on the Great South Bay,
on my father's ketch, a reef in the main,
south wind bristling, sun whipping off
his face, the rail skimming the water,
my mother frightened we will tip,
my father pushing it so far
you can hear the mast groan.

I laid quietly on deck
watching the water eat
through the gunnels, believing
it was the voice of God coming alive.
It was the only time my father was his joy,
the only time my mother was her fear.

Not once did I ever think we would tip.
I look at this Chinese junk, forty years later,
in an old book, on a windy day, hours from
the sea, and I know for the first time,
we could have.

Still, I count this blindness a gift.
And something in me has spent my life
leaning into the water. Though today,
I am sad for how my mother
was pushed to the edge.

THE EDGE

They had traveled a long way,
each from a beginning the others
couldn't imagine. When they
reached the edge, they all peered
deeply, as far as they could.

Almost at once, they gasped
and held onto each other. Then,
one declared, "I knew it. Beyond,
there is nothing." Another countered,
"For me, it holds everything." By now,
the fearful one fretted, "I knew I should
never have come." Dizzied by the view,
he retreated, "I must go back."

Finally, the blind one poked his way
to the edge and after a while sighed,
"It's as I've always known."

It was too late to travel down and so
they were forced to listen to each other
through the night.

The blind one began, "What will you
bring back?" The one who saw nothing
said, "That where we are is all there
is. That's what I'll say."

The one who saw everything smiled,
"I'll bear witness that we are cradled
by something incomprehensible."

At this, the fearful one jumped in,
"Well, my advice will be
to just stay put."

In the silence that followed,
they asked the blind one who
confessed, "I'm not going back."

WHITE TEA

They say I've been delirious.
I tell them I am nothing
if not loved. They tell
me to rest. I drink from
their heads and they heal
me with their prayers
boiled down like tea.

I sleep, I think.
They come back and offer
themselves to be plucked and
powdered and steamed.

The aroma of their eyes
breaks my loneliness.
I drink them down.

I look away. They say
a day has passed. The nurse
brings a cup of faces I have
known. I drink them down.
My fear steams away.

That night, a wind moves
through the cave I've been hiding
in. I fight off sleep, but the wind
takes my song.

I look away. A week they say.
The fever is up. They bring

another cup and the long fingers
of the wind that have my song
dig down in me beneath
what is ill.

BASEMENTS AND DREAMS

Not very far apart. Searching, in Brooklyn, when a boy, through my grandfather's books, half in languages I didn't even recognize, edges torn, pages missing. I've always been drawn to the missing pages. As if all my instructions have been waiting there. In a musty corner in Brooklyn, I found his Talmud. I hold it now, more artifact than book, and pray more than read it. And later, still a boy, in my father's basement among all the lathes and chisels and saws. Sawdust everywhere. He always feverishly building something. As if he were secretly mitering the foundation of some yet to be discovered Pyramid. I never got too close. He never really wanted help. But still, it was the only place in our home that was what it seemed. He was too busy creating to be anything but real. I used to sit on the wooden steps between worlds: listening to my mother upstairs trying to remove the stains of life, while my father pushed the whir of tools, opening wood in the underworld of our tense, unspoken lives. And then all the basements of oncology in my thirties, being wheeled through unfinished hallways, floors below the more acceptable practices. It was in the hushed and sterile basement of Albany Med that my eighth rib was removed and dropped in a jar that no one knew what to do with. And all I've written through the years, packed in boxes and carried from state to state, from self to emerging self, waiting for the clarity of heart to know what to do with all the missing pages and the voices that have spoken them. That's what this is really about. About the furnace of lineage, burning through and up just in time. About letting birds of fire fly from the basement of my heart. About unpacking the sacred texts that can never be spoken anyway. And now, after dying and coming back, it's really not about my books, but about the voice beneath my name keeping the song going. Now this dream in my 53rd year where my old dead mentor is telling me to take my books out of the basement. There, among them, a totem, a carved Tibetan figure with a wooden flame coming out of his head. I know that flame, have felt it for years. It took almost dying to realize that, though it comes through me, it is not mine. Like the fire at the center of the earth. Like the fire at the center of us all. Awake and on fire just in time. It seems my sufferings have burned the coverings from my eyes just in time. . .

THE FRIEND

There is a friend older than birth
who danced with you before you had a body,
a friend who stays close to your life, the way
heat stays close to a flame. Can you feel it?
I know, it's hard. I often turn and it's gone.

But you may have seen it in the glow
that remains for those few seconds after you
turn the light off. Or in the ache that beats
in your blood after you turn away
from something you love.

We each have a friend older than birth,
more patient than the ocean, more giving
than the rain, a place of high safety
waiting like a nest of song whenever
we are ready.

All we have to do is put down the many
things we believe we have to carry, put down
everything we've worked for, not deny it or
curse it, but simply undo our grip, simply
untie our need to have it last.

If we can't, the friend will wait
until we die, when it will carry our pain
like seed into God, the way that song swallows
smoke when no one's looking. But while alive,
if we can find what's alive, the friend will
stretch its honeyed thread between our
heart and eye to sweeten what we know.

Yes, there is a friend older than birth
who dislikes mirrors, but adores windows.

And when you look upon something with
love and close your eyes, the trace of light
you see is the litmus of the Divine, and all
you love, all you see with love, all you hold
in your heart after love—all are images that
the friend carves on the cave of your soul, for
the times you fall down and are forced
to look within.

MORE DREAMS

Last week, walking a pier
to a surly physician's office,
his hands smelling of bait.

He threw his knife
on the desk and said my skull
was aging faster than the rest.
I protested. He started beheading
catfish, "There's nothing we can do."

I stormed out. The uncertain race
was on. Why is my skull aging? Too much
fire in my head? Not enough flow?

I woke determined to find a doctor
who would say I would not die.

I woke with this thickened sensation
along the back of my head where the tumor
had been. Had been. Had been. Say it.

I am well.

Without telling anyone,
I've made a secret of running
water on my head.

REQUIEM FOR A FATHER MISSING

1. SAVING BONDS

I am preparing to be honest with my father, not about anything particular, but about the basic situation of being his son, of being the recipient of his constant prodding. I am trying out scenes, occasions to talk to him, to tell him how I feel. With trepidation, I plan a trip for us. We drive into Brooklyn to see my Grandmother, to take care of her bills and to transfer some of her banking.

As we drive the turnpike, I start to speak when he interrupts, questioning if I have all the right papers and numbers. He's squinting at the wheel. He never lets me drive. When I try to talk about something of importance, he always interrupts with some practical interrogation.

"Did you get the account numbers from your mother?" he blurts out. I sigh, "No." He gets angry and critical. I say, "We can call when we get there." He won't let it drop. He barks, "We need the bonds!" I say flatly, "All we have to do is ask." We begin to argue.

It seems quite telling that we are after a way to save bonds which Grandma holds. We never agree on how to do so. I start to tell him that he never listens or asks any questions. He interrupts with a shot of anger, "The only reason you write all that Art is 'cause you don't have the courage to talk to me."

The ride goes nowhere. That night I dream of a time when he is older. I am reluctantly walking up a path to a small suburban home in which my father, in his eighties or nineties, is living by himself. Apparently my mother has died. As I open the screen door, I realize I am performing a rather routine visit, checking on him, though it is never a pleasant task. Once inside, the place is small, dark, and dusty. The windows are neither open nor closed, the drapes half-drawn. I whisper hello and ask how he's doing. There is only a short grumble from a hunched figure huddled under a blanket on the couch. He is completely covered with no part of his body showing. I sense no fear beneath the blanket, just utter isolation. It seems tragically clear that this is the cold summit of his self-centered ways. I sit beside him and pull the blanket from his face. His angry eyes are unfocused in their stare. It is uncomfortable to look at him, though I don't look away. I ask if I can do anything. He mumbles, " . . . milk."

It breaks my own anger to realize that there is nothing I can say that will ever penetrate the horror he has encased himself in. My want for him to acknowledge all he's done evaporates. Looking into these spiritless eyes, I can only see his endless agitation. I back away from the couch and wake feeling entirely too harsh to him.

2. THE ULTIMATE CRAFTSMAN

When the tumor on my brain was swelling like bad fruit, you sat across from me in the middle of the day and you took my hand. You had never done that. I still remember the cool roughness of hands that have loved wood better. You were, still are, the ultimate craftsman. But there were no tools for this. You took my hand and quivered, "I would take your place, if I could." I wanted to cry. You did. In that moment, I felt like your son. I felt some rarely touched part of you reach all the way back to when you and Mom wanted a son. I know in that moment you were there—wanting to have me—and here—about to lose me. I'd waited so long for something tender from you but when it came, I was afraid to trust it. I couldn't let you in.

A year later, when I was throwing up from chemo in a Holiday Inn twenty minutes from the house I grew up in, you wouldn't come. My mother said no, and you didn't speak your heart. You didn't say, "That's my son. Get out of the way." I sat on the floor of that motel room in a puddle of hell while you had dry toast, watching your cholesterol. Part of my heart broke off and fell in some dark crack. I've never gotten it back. From that day, one thread blackened and another snapped.

3. LIKE AN OLD FISH

I am now 46. You are 77. I have left a marriage after twenty years. I am living with myself. I am watching the snow drift outside my apartment, clinging to bare limbs of trees I'm befriending. I feel close to these trees, for I am as bare, finally. Able to feel the slight-press-of-being-alive touch me and burst into clearness like a flake of wonder that falls from nowhere. In the midst of all this, you call, your voice shaky and uncertain. You were never good on the phone. You always let Mom speak for you. Something I've had to overcome myself. It is not a sound way. But you call and I feel the deep risk it takes for you. I tell you I love you. You're much more fragile now that your hair has lost all color. You're thin and your hearing is going, though you won't admit it. You say in all seriousness that it's only the high-pitch sounds, like women's voices, that you have trouble hearing. You utter briefly that you don't know how it all happened this way and you begin to cry. I cry slowly without a sound on the other end. You're whispering as if in secret, as if my mother might return any minute and you will have to go underground. I fear you'll never really know how I treasure your courage and sweetness in this moment. It is not very much over a lifetime between a father and a son, but it is everything. It is all that we have managed. Afterwards, I stare at the phone so long I think your stuttered heart is trapped in it, like an old fish in a very small tank.

4. ON MY OWN

When I was nine and the bully chased me into our yard, I ran, fast as I could, for the door, for home, for refuge. My throat swelled when I tried the metal knob and it wouldn't turn. I tried again, could hear the bully getting closer. It wouldn't turn. When I looked up through the screen, there you were, stern and forbidding, telling me to fight my own battles. Heart pounding, I ran into our yard and stopped. The bully arrived, fists flying. I remember being hit in the back and tucked myself so as not to be hit in the face. I tumbled to the ground. From this wasted position, I could see you watching through that locked screen door as blow after blow kept hammering my back. Each blow was a chance for you to save me. No matter how it hurt, I wouldn't let you see me cry. I can't remember how it all ended, what made the other boy go home. I only remember that you wouldn't stop it. From that moment, I was on my own. I couldn't afford to be a child any longer. I hated having to try that screen door again, all bruised and scratched, afraid it would still be locked. Hated slinking back into that house, you nowhere to be seen. Hated that the only place I had to go was through that door. We've never mentioned it, not to this day.

5. SLABS AND PLANKS

I was teaching on a lake in upstate New York four hundred miles away, when I learned you had a stroke. It was mild, the only trace now, a small stone under your tongue. Your *s*'s are slabs instead of razors. Your *t*'s are planks instead of glass. I drove right away, warning myself that the threat of death wouldn't change anything, but hoping nonetheless. I called you from the road, and you wept into the phone. You were panicked. Your speech was full of large stones. I could hear through the phone that everyone was a walking siren. My brother was hysterical. It was as if no one in our family had ever gone through anything, as if my dying and coming back was invisible. But now, my finely tuned heart, which you had made fun of for years, was sorely needed. Go figure.

I came with no expectation but the big one. I came really for the moment when I would first see you in your hospital bed, all broken open and humbled. I moved steadily through the sterile halls, gathering the hospital smells like memories of a solitary war. I pulled the curtain and lifted you in my arms. You cried like a small child, your tears all over my face. You touched me the deepest when you couldn't speak. As I let you go, my brother, atremble and bent, collapsed in your thin, white arms. It was then I realized. When I held you, I was the father. When you held him, he was held by his father. How could this have happened? I have always been the father.

I drove the four hundred miles back and walked a soft and merciless lake at night, and told a stranger how my father loves the sea. It's the only thing we really share, and when it feels like you're already dead, because of things never lifted between us, I sometimes find a slow shore very early or very late and imagine you beside me. I am lonely father, all by myself in the immense wonder. Can't you walk with me? Can't we kneel beside each other like small stumps washed ashore, our knots bleached, our centers hollowed, our edges broken by the many times we've failed to touch?

6. DREAM 75

My father is behind the wheel, in his pajamas, driving Susan and me to have hot dogs by the Bay. He smiles deeply and says this is his favorite thing to do. Somehow, it's clear that he has Alzheimers. I realize it's not safe to let him drive. I gently take the wheel from the passenger side, steering us slowly to the side of the road. Just then, everything becomes extremely icy and we start sliding out of control. Cars are gently crashing into each other all around us, like the bumper cars at Coney Island when I was a boy. Thankfully, we land in a driveway and I decide that we'll wait out the ice.

The scene shifts and I meet him years later, though he doesn't know who I am. He asks, and I, not saying I'm his son, let him know I am a poet. He seems mildly interested. I offer to take him to have a hot dog by the Bay. His smile broadens, "Hey, that's one of my favorite things to do." I take him by the elbow, "Huh, me too."

FOR THREE VOICES LOST IN FLIGHT

But in the glass parade,
who should I praise?
Those who need the truth,
though they can never tell it?
Or those who will not search,
though they are always honest?
Or those formed by their call,
though they never share it?

After all the yellow turns of thirst,
I cannot say. Only this.
There is no limit to what I can give,
thank God, the lesson at end of youth,
for as age ordains, there is no limit
to what can be asked.

OPENING WITHOUT WORDS

It is the beginning of May
and over near the statue of Moses,
raising his staff to something
none of us can see, hundreds of tulips
have broken through the dark earth
becoming every color they held inside
and quietly they ignore each other
in this chorus of oneness, bobbing gently,
as children race up to their splashes
of yellow and red, expecting the colors
to sing, and maybe they do in a song
only children can hear, and old men
amble through the rows, hands behind
their backs, as if in some European church
about to crumble, and this old white-haired
woman, with sheer wonder on her face,
sneaks up on the pink ones, her silent mouth
a flower, and, for the moment, we are all
opening without words, and her dog,
a pink-nosed spaniel drops its ball
and rolls on its back slowly, and
Susan jumps out of her shoes,
pulls me by my sun-warmed hand
into the middle of a yellow patch,
buries her face in them and rises,
a color breaking ground herself,
pollen on her nose. Quietly,
we are saved, again.

PERIL

I was feeling
not broken, not whole,
not able to finish or begin.

And not dreaming,
but certainly not awake,
I trudged some dry and rolling plain;
not dunes, not earth; not clumped,
not sand; scrubby but with
slender trees of reed.

And in the dip,
a prehistoric bison,
milk-white,
its belly soiled.
It reared its horn
and turned for me.

I began to run.
It brushed me, swift and warm.
I stumbled back and there were bones,
a baked animal jaw, a browned lower rib,
like that from a cow. I hurled
the jaw at it.

It knocked me to the ground.
Then trotted to its safe-point
and worked its head my way.

The trees of reed rustled.
And breathing fast, it began to glow,

its head snorting the air, its neck
sheer lineament and muscle.

The thing then slimmed or tensed,
evolving into something rideable,
all vein and light,
not quite a horse.

But irresistible,
it waited for me
to mount.

I woke afraid.
And now, it seems
unfindable.

INCH OF KARMA

How a woman who worships her body,
who even when in love watches the press
of her breast and never the mouth that
sucks from it, how she at 55 should
skid off a road near Denver and wake
with a scar snaking through her breasts,
how she can't bear to look at herself,
how she thinks tomorrow itches like a scar,
how she should sit next to me this golden
afternoon claiming herself a tragedy.

How 500 days past my brain tumor
and five days from my rib tumor
I take her wrist and think,
"Can you walk and speak?"
How she senses this and says,
"I know I'm vain." I squeeze her
wrist and say nothing. How she
gives me her other wrist, anxious
to have me hatch her truth
against her will.

How I wonder, who am I to minimize
her pain? How she wants me to minimize
her pain. How the Universe improvises
its balance. How a horse thief becomes a
horse. How a blacksmith becomes an anvil.
How my surgeon will become a gardener.

How the wings of one life are broken
to form a nest in which someone is born

who can go everywhere
while going nowhere.

How I envy that.

How I've asked for so long
to see with the freshness of the
first man, and how I've had to
give up a rib in order to go on.

How the obstacles will
shape us if we let them.
How I ache for someone
to minimize my pain.

How I'd like to run away
but can't, for I must
have done that once before.

.

NOTE ON THE FRIDGE FOR YOU

You asked a profound question last night, when you asked about death. One that people who love each other never answer, but invite to the table like a relative who lives far away, but who moves closer through the years. When you asked, I turned quiet and we fell into making love. Not because I was avoiding the question, but because, for all I've been through and all I've written, loving is the best answer I know. But I want to talk with you about this, not just once, but for the rest of our lives, until death surfaces, at first as a cloud on a sunny day, and eventually, as a burst of light that breaks through a cloudy day. I know that sounds impossible, but I have felt both, sometimes at once. I have no particular wisdom about this. Just that almost dying has carved me a third eye that sometimes sees, but which often waters until I see nothing. I know death is with me often, nearby, over my shoulder, and the trick, if there is one, is to feel its insistence on how precious everything is without turning around too much, getting caught in its stare. It has made me look for eternity inside your eyes, in the silence of the willow, in our dog's sleepy breathing—rather than in the field of unlived years. It has wiped me clean, not stripped of fear, but humbled into joy, to be up before the sun, eager for the day, for when you wake, for how our dog comes to let you know that the coffee is ready. Pour a cup. I'm upstairs. Come. We can die to the silence and listen.

ON ONE CORNER
(IN BARCELONA)

Two angels stand, poised, frozen
like weathered statues, even their faces
are covered with mottled paint, and
for a coin the smaller one will bless you.

At first, everyone smiles and laughs.
"They're very good," one tourist says, but
then a child, no more than eight, rushes up
with a coin her mother gave her, and she
looks up with such awe, that even the
beautiful young woman painted as an
angel believes, for the moment, that
she has something to bestow.

Her eyes sparkle through the paint
and she blesses the child. The street is
hushed. The small child bows and scampers
into her life. The noise resumes and the dirty
angels freeze, becoming statues again.

The crowd leaves and I ache
to be blessed as I fumble
for a coin.

LADDERS TO NOWHERE

The storm mounts and with little
warning engulfs us. The only safe
place is inside the tunnel of wind.

Human storms are no different.
They circle us with a violence
that rips about a still center.

When hurt, it is tempting
to reach into the storm for
what we have been denied.

But one touch at that velocity
and we are yanked into the in-
satiable wall of desire breaking
everything in its path.

No matter how much you
deserve what is whipping by,
the only thing to do is to
stay in the center.

TALKIN' ABOUT EVERYTHING

We carry it around so near we don't see it.
And everything—the gust that wakes
the trees, the laugh that breaks my
distance—each sweet advance of life
blows up our skirt and says, "Come on,
I'm talkin' about everything here!"

Often, we need to fall to see
that every small thing hides its beauty
in its smallness, for beauty is shy.
Tripped or knocked down, we are forced
to stay with it, to bow to it.

Take the eye of someone close, someone
you see every day. Or your own. If we could look
into that holy pool for more than a few seconds,
we would fall through. Or the room of some-
one dying. If we could settle into the silence
beneath our fear, we'd come to the
shore between life and death and
simply hold each other.

This all started when watching a squirrel
eat from our feeder. We'd bought one
designed to keep that squirrel out. And
then my wife said, "They have to eat, too."

So now I'm thinking, we spend so much time
devising ways to keep things out. But aren't
we all that squirrel desperate to eat at God's
feeder? Beneath the veil, our lips grow
soft enough to kiss everything.

THE SALT OF OUR HISTORY

The net is more important
than the fish. It is the casting,
the waiting, the pull, not knowing
what is resisting. And the fact
that every good net has holes
is a reminder that everything
that lands in our hands
is just a borrowing.

After burning our hands,
things too big must be
returned, too.

And we who cast
are netted and let go
as well.

When we are caught,
we pray to slip through.
When we slip through,
we pray to be lifted.

And God is just
an invisible fisherman
burning us with soul
before throwing us back.

Weak Enough

Sometimes in sickness,
we are weak enough to enter heaven.

— Robert Lowell

DIAPEDESIS

—the passing of blood through
intact bloodwalls,
from the Greek, "a leaping
through"

As I waited
to be wheeled
after surgery,
my head enlarging
where they'd entered,
the white shuffling
seemed so pure, mute
angels with masks
instead of wings.
I was tagged and
left to cool.

Then rolled
through halls
like a broken fish
urged back upstream
by all the pudgy fishermen
who having pulled me
changed their mind.

I was throbbing in the hall,
when my oldest friends, half
upside down, caressed my face
and arms. The stretcher rolled
the sandy floor. Their touch
made me thirsty.

Now, in my room,
on my wing, a cruel name
for beds of broken fish,
my head pounds.
And other selves
keep wheeling by.

The lights go down,
the suffering glows
and the nurses shift
the glowing side up.
Then send us off
and trash
the syringe.

STRANGE AND BEAUTIFUL
(FOR WAYNE)

Life is so beautiful.
It's the living that can be strange.

Just ask the root growing in the mud.
Or the snail thrown back by surf.

Or ask your other, the one you
no longer talk to, who grows confused
just when everything feels possible.

Or see yourself in me. For you
are a possibility I always return to.
When no one's looking, the light
of the world blinds me as it
flickers through the break
in your heart.

HOW TO MOURN A MIRACLE

There are so many I should be
calling, thanking, writing long
thoughtful letters to. But I feel
so wispy, like a robe of myths
baking on a dock while what
wore me swims upstream.

And what would I say?
I've been away and now
I'm home? That their care—
don't ask me how—has made it
safe again? At dinner, I drop
my fork, unable to drop my thoughts.
In the hospital, the forks were
bent and spotted. I feel my organs
all the time. They speak to me.

Why does light stop me now?
When seeing the blood of a sunny
day melt the grass, I am crushed.
Why is everything
I want to say red?

WHILE I WAS THERE

1. FEBRUARY 1984

The day begins by dusting a heavy snow off the windshield before the sun comes up, then playing raquetball against a very huge man who always beats me. After donuts and coffee, I go home, leave the garage door open, and rush to answer the phone. It is my mother. She doesn't say it right away, but I know something is wrong.

Grandma is in the hospital. Wednesday evening she began to have chest pains around eleven. By one-thirty, she was scared and called Mom and Dad. Grandma is my father's mother. She lives in Brooklyn, in the four-family house they bought in 1922, when my father was two. She's lived there for sixty-two years. How I'd rummage through their basement. It was a musty passageway to a more ancient world. The creaking of each step grew louder as the warm noise of Grandma's broken English would slip softer.

That basement was an early teacher. It oozed presence. Through the yellowed piles of *Life* magazines and *National Geographics* from the 1940s. Through that row of storage bins which seemed like an urban manger. Through the stacks of leather bound, gold-leaf books with gnarled bindings. Through the torn and pasted wall of *Esquire* nudes my father and his brother put up as kids. And the sloped doors to the yard which in summer seemed like the upper world that Plato's freed agent of the cave surfaced into. All of this cemented passion to curiosity for me. It made me accept, at an early age, without the awareness to draw strength from such an understanding, that knowledge was some dark and ancient basement pulsating beneath the noise of the world. This was where musty smells drew me—to feel the flapping storage bin of a basement in Brooklyn as the damp ventricle of the Universe.

When I'd surface through the sloped doors into their tiny yard, lethargic neighbors would stare in their t-shirts and robes in a way that stopped me from sharing what I'd found. I'd run back inside and rush through the basement, up the stairs into the first-floor apartment warm with the smell of potato pancakes and weak tea. And Grandma would light up to see her dead husband's Talmud in my hands.

But Grandma is in the hospital. This is the second time in two months. Her left valve is calcifying and the blood can't leave her heart as smoothly, can't flow as cleanly as it once had. That's the source of her pain, the blood not flowing freely.

I am afraid Grandma will die, not before I get there, but while I am there. I have just typed all the poems I have written for her but never given her. Now I'm wondering whether to shower them on her bed or to hide them in her basement. How will she feel about all that I've written? Mom said she has tubes in her nose and is being fed intravenously. I wonder what that would feel like, clear tubes up my nose.

Grandma is 88 and her very large heart is starting to lumber and congest. Before it fails, she is being advised to have open-heart surgery. Though she is strong, there is significant risk in having such an operation at her age. Yet I'm afraid if she dies without trying, she will have fallen too, will have succumbed to the pessimism and thwarted attitude my parents parade around in. It means everything to me that she not give up. It rips a secret place in my heart to think of her coming all this way from Russia—through the Depression, through the Holocaust, and the complacent abuses that the elderly face in modern America—to give up and wait to die. I fear my heart will fail if she gives up. I know this imposition is all mine. Still, it is working me.

When I went to see her in November, walking down 33rd Street, passing the brick apartment buildings, I had to side-step two sassy, sensuous, precocious, leathered, tight-pants kids dancing and smoking to a music box on the roof of a stranger's car. I rang the buzzer whose label she printed before I was born. As I sat with her at her kitchen table, she told me of being a child in Katarinaslav outside of Kiev. She called the land fat, and told how her father would wake them to drink warm milk from a goat and they would groggily go back to sleep. To see her face drift into her past, into the circle of all her dead—I would have given anything to keep her there, to prevent her from surfacing in the rubble of the Brooklyn street that lined her daily walk to the senior citizen center. When I left, I came close to crying two or three times in the subway back to Manhattan, could feel the train speed through the dark like truth toward the future, could see her watching soaps, peeling potatoes, and polishing the brass mailbox covers in the hallway, though the building is no longer hers.

But this is February, and Grandma is in the hospital and, on the way to see her, my father says how he wishes his father could see how she speaks English now. Nehemiah was a printer and always wanted Grandma to speak English. But she resisted. Dad says she hardly spoke English at all while his father was alive. She'd be charming and articulate at social gatherings, but in dealing with the world, or when feeling misunderstood, she'd insist on speaking Yiddish. Mom says, "She was never this strong when he was alive." My mother shakes her head, "Her will, which wouldn't speak English, is the same stubbornness that's going to have the operation."

2. NOVEMBER 2005

Grandma had the operation. She spread her 88 year old heart before them like thick halves of a salmon that had crossed the ocean of her life. They put her to sleep, cleaned it out, and put her back together. She lived another six years. She never lost her accent or her strength, though she spent the rest of her days in Kingsbrook Medical Center in Brooklyn. And when I would drive the three hundred miles to see her, she would beam as I crossed into her small room, revert back to Yiddish, sometimes Russian, and think I was Nehemiah. She would take my hand and mutter some private things in a language I could barely enter, then drift off with a sigh. I would simply hold her weathered hands and feel privileged to slip into my grandfather's skin for a moment or two. And as she began to sleep, I would whisper of the fat land of Katarinaslav and conjure her to recall the warm goat's milk that her father would cup for her just before dawn. At this, she always smiled and turned groggy.

When Grandma died, I thought I'd lost an anchor in the world. I had no idea she was just slipping into me more completely. Now I see her face less but feel her presence more. She lived like a working angel whose large heart served as the weight that kept her tied to the earth, no matter how hard she pumped her dreams. At first I thought this sad. But having worked my own beautiful weight, I now know it is simply perfect.

FOR THE ONE WHO MISSES LAUGHTER

You arrive after years like a bird with a broken beak.
You are finally a breath away from everything.
You ask if there's a poem for you.
Of course, there is a poem in everything.
The whole way home I search for what it might be.

I send this now as a mirror, for the poem is in
the crack along your beak. So go outside and let
the sun spill through the crack into your heart.
Can you feel it? That quiver in your throat?

It's the quiver of your soul, gasping like a swimmer
held under too long. Though you have betrayed it,
it will never betray you.

Let the sun flood the crack till it illuminates
the poem which is the pain that brought you here.
It is our teacher.

A VOW BEYOND AWARENESS

Knowing others have wanted to move the world
and were forced to accept how the world moved them,
that others have suffered as much, that some have grown
too hard for it, while some have weakened into bliss;
knowing the winter field with sunlit stalks holds a
secret for each life outlasting the cold, that thousands
have called out to God in their most private despair
long before we were even born, that the wisdom
in silence and water has received them all; knowing
the spark we call love has made sane men soft and
determined women reconsider, that the with-
holding of love has sent flowers into exile, that
the long breath of one star consumes a hundred
generations; knowing how little and how much
one speck of dream accounts for, and how
easy it is to let the want of others take over;
knowing when misunderstood how quickly
we can swallow the rush of anything spiritual,
and how common the weight of having to make
due; knowing how much is at stake, it is imperative
to close our knowing, as a cliff diver closes his
eyes, and live—as if no one had ever
lived before.

HEARING GOOD ADVICE

Everyone is after me
to stay positive, but
tonight I feel like
pissing on a rock,
like hearing good
advice and doing
nothing.

Everyone wants me
to kick ass, though
I don't know
what to kick.

They say I'm
too quiet, but words
taste like armor.

I want to be
with my Godchild
who is obsessed
with the moon,
who is too young
to speak.

I want to be obsessed
with a rock of light
that rises through the dark.

FIVE THOUSAND WAYS TO LISTEN
(IN BARCELONA)

I don't know Spanish. So listening to everyone is like moving through a field of birds forced by the wind to fly, each singing at the light and looking for each other.

We have come to be in dialogue with a group of Spaniards and the translator is so adept that he listens to their whole story before putting it into English. I find myself listening beyond the noise of our words: to the tilt of a head, the wince of a heart, the sudden laughter at self-recognition, the lifting of hands, the silent stare when they fall off of what they mean to say. · And though I don't understand a thing they are saying, we understand each other.

Moments keep spilling open and, though we can't make sense of each other's words, we also can't hide behind them, but must reach for something in between. And in this reaching, God waits to be aroused.

As the conversation winds down, the father of our translator starts to speak. It is clear he is sharing something very personal. Slowly, his son begins to translate, "My father says he has a mental illness and it has prevented him from loving his family well. He takes pills now, but doubts if he'll ever be cured. He suffers greatly and feels ashamed."

There is a long silence and the Spanish father who trips in and out of his mind is searching with his troubled eyes beneath the floor as we wait to see what he will unearth. Finally, he utters something, sounding like an ox under a heavy load. His gentle son tells us, "My father says, 'Sometimes, my suffering is greater than my shame and I must speak.' "

Someone blurts out a stream of Spanish. The son translates, "There are two ways to free the heart: the breaking in of suffering or the flying out of love." The words puff and sink into our silence like stones thrown into the sea.

That evening, we are drawn into stories of our own fathers, and I fall into the tale of my mother's father from Rumania, one of six sons scattered across the globe. That night, he comes to me in a dream. I rush into his arms, as I did when a boy, shouting, "Poppi! Poppi!" He hugs me, then strokes my cheek and says, "Stop with these big, big stories. I was just a man."

THE CROWS BETWEEN US

You are 84. I am 53. We haven't talked in eight years.
These are facts. But I am now the age you were when I had
cancer, and this very night, at 2 a.m., your wife's voice comes to me
in dream. We are on the phone and she won't tell me the truth.
I press her. Finally, after a silence that sends ten crows out of the
tree between us, she says, "Your father is going to die soon." I wake,
unsure what to do. I've called for you my whole life and you could
never break away. Death feels like just another shore I won't be able
to find. I check my machine and there's a message but no words.
I think to call my brother, but realize he won't know. I am all alone,
the crows are lost, and your heart is torn exactly where mine is.
The last time we spoke you cried on the phone but wouldn't see
me. I cry in my sleep constantly. These are strange jurisdictions.
You wanted me to come into this world, then circled me like
a fire you could never understand. I taught you how to hug
and loved your mother more than my own. I listened to you
repeat yourself for hours on rain-warped benches while our
wives would hunt for bargains. I listened and studied the lines
in your face. You never came when I was throwing up from chemo.
You never came when I said I'd meet you anywhere. And now, it
had to happen, you've grown old, and everyone keeps asking if
I want to see you before you die. I don't know if there's any point
in my coming, though I'm up in the night pounding again for
answers to the pain that is you. You were never able to listen
or ask. Neither of you. It wasn't that you were busy, more like
your faces were held under by some unnamable force in a river
of agitation that you blamed on everyone you met. I wish I could
hold you. Is there any chance that when you die this pain will stop?
I will always love you. And the sea. I thank you for the sea. It's where
I've looked for you. It's where I've found myself. It's now 4 a.m. and
I lie down, thinking if you can send me this, I can send pebbles of

truth into the waters of your dream. I close my eyes and press the
ridge in my heart where I keep you. I can see you sleeping in your
room and I repeat without words . . . though we are unresolved,
we are alright. You can go, if you need to. We are alright.
There's been too much pain and the crows are lost,
but we are alright, father. You can go . . .
We are alright . . .

FIRES LOOKING FOR A SEA

She was an old cellist. Behind her was
a waterfall, thin, steady, gentle, much
like her. She was playing Bach, and slowly,
I could feel the bow rubbing the strings, could
feel her hand pushing the bow, could feel her
heart pushing her hand, her eyes closed,
drawing on the suffering and joy
of a long life.

And opened like that, it occurred to me
that the rubbing of strings until they
produce music is as good a way as
any to describe the thinning
between inner and outer.

All my life I've tried to lessen what stands
between my heart and the world, between my
mind and the sky, between my eye and your eye.
Never realizing that when who we are is our skin,
well, yes, we can know the inside of mystery. We
might even glimpse the face of God. But we also
live like burn survivors screaming at the air.
This too is part of being awake, this being
on fire, always looking for a sea.

This is why my wife cries at the deer
sleeping in the snow. Why she wants
to touch the flakes on their closed lids.

The old cellist played before the waterfall
and everyone slouched, till somewhere inside,

our hearts thinned like strings and our minds
worked like bows.

Ever since, I feel the living skin of heart
laying itself bare before the draw
and rub of beauty.

We want so badly to be awake, never
knowing the art that waits, when there
is nowhere left to hide.

EARTH GUEST

We are all just guests in a body
that comes and goes. When on
the verge of leaving that body,
it becomes clear—there
is a flame in everything.

If I look long enough, I can see
the flicker in the meat of a tree
and this morning I see it
in the slender throat of a doe
nibbling through early mist.

If still enough, I can hear
the flame at the center of the earth
which nothing can contain—
yes, flowers are just licks of flame
breaking through in spring.

It's the same in you and me,
in every stranger afraid to speak,
a small pilot light that no one
can put out, and love and truth
make it burn brighter
and we call the brightness joy.

But if you want to see
the small living flame itself,
well, that's strange business.
It's somewhat like the stars—
it's always there

but only seeable
in the dark.

It's why the heart,
when least expected,
glows like a candle
in each moment
of despair.

FOR THE CIRCLE

A friend is a second self.
— *Cicero*

We are all changed.
You, for reaching through this fire
that wanted me, so far
that parts of you
are fixed in me
like glass in tar.

I'm sorry, and not,
that you were burned
for holding me.

Each of us, scorched
beyond the dream line.

Cancer with all its worms
made us peel the masks.

What a painful and glorious way
to better oneself.

HOWARD IS MY BROTHER

Martin was Howard's closest friend. I used to envy their friendship, though I was so different from them. As for Martin, he was one of the most genuine beings to gallop across my youth. He was simple and well-defined in a classical, Greek way. He aspired to be good, thoughtful, and helpful. Not much else to it. He was like Steinbeck's Lenny in *Of Mice and Men*, except with grace and intelligence.

I am ten months older than Howard. And so, he often felt overshadowed by my involvement in school with girls and the social scene. But he was more mature. He was somehow immune to the torturous, adolescent need for approval, only to battle for our parents' approval as he got older. But early on, he somehow knew the feel of true friendship; while I had to search for it, clumsily, through acquaintance after acquaintance, discovering more often than not what friendship wasn't.

There were times I felt jealous of Martin usurping my position as brother. I was popular, but alone. Whenever my crowd would stand me up—forget to call or get me—I would ask if I could play with Howard and Martin. My mother always said, "It's up to them." Howard was always annoyed, but he never said no. I never recognized this as the innate kindness it was. I would simply be momentarily relieved from my loneliness and try to win Martin over to me. Those were childish ways and I'm a long way from childhood to have only acknowledged them now.

Well, Martin joined the Marines while in college and went one summer to Paris Island to train as a Green Beret. He came home, knocking on our door, looking sixty pounds thinner and thoroughly beaten. We all laughed, though I could see how concerned Howard was. Martin went on to tell us, with great charm and an ability to snicker at himself, of the things he was asked to do to ready himself for war. How he was one of five hundred men standing at attention in a set of bleachers, having to chant rhymes of discipline while passing a poisonous snake. Within the next year, Martin married a thin pale Southern Belle who was the daughter of a Colonel or something. He went on to become a Captain of a unit of MPs in West Germany where, with two children and a third on the way, he died at the age of thirty-one, in three days, of spinal meningitis.

Howard was married to Chris by this time and creating a home of his own. He was checking our house, on the spur of the moment, because Mom and Dad were in Maryland visiting Uncle Irwin, when the phone rang. Strangely, it was Martin's mother calling to tell my parents that Martin had died. Howard wasn't even supposed to be there. He was run over. He called my parents in Maryland and Mom, misunderstanding him in his tears, thought that I had died. When it was all cleared up, she was relieved it was Martin. At the time, I had never felt another's loss so completely. Martin had been violently ripped from him. For the first time in our lives, Howard needed me. I asked him stay with us. He brought Chris.

The first night, after dinner, while Ann and Chris were in the kitchen, he sat on our shorter couch and began to weep. He said, "The thing I can't get out of my mind is how cold Martin must be in the ground." Howard waited after the funeral, till everyone left, to say good-bye but couldn't do it. He put his head in his hands and kept weeping. He couldn't believe that, just like that, over the phone, his dearest friend, closer to him than his own brother, was dead. He was weeping in cascades, "I never even got to say good-bye." I held him and said, "You don't need to respond to what I'm going to say, but I want you to know that I will always be there for you."

He didn't respond but from that moment on, we began to treat each other as brothers. Through all of this, I've come to understand the anxiety with which my brother lives. He has been more brutally influenced by my parents than me and is a worrier. I am the stronger parts of my mother. He is the weaker. They are so much alike in certain ways that they repel each other.

About a year after Martin's death, my mother in a phone conversation admitted that, "Howard really shouldn't have called that night. After all, there was nothing we could have done, being in Maryland. He could've waited till we got back. It kinda put a damper on the whole weekend." I hung up and stared at the phone. It's something I've done a lot in my life, stare at the phone.

Years later—when I was wrung out from my first chemo treatment, bruised and emaciated; when I vowed never to let anyone ever put another needle in my arm, no matter what—it was Howard who called. It started out awkwardly as he tried to convince me to keep taking those treatments. I resisted. We couldn't hear each other and the call ended badly. Then, while staring at the phone, he called back. His voice was trembling. He was naked now, stuttering toward me, "Please, I'll come and sit with you . . . Just keep getting better . . . I'll do whatever you want . . ." I will always love him for that.

It's eighteen years from that call, and twenty-two years from the time that Martin died. Howard and Chris have a daughter, Brooke, who is going to be eighteen. And I live in Michigan with Susan. They, in New York. I'm not sure what's happened along the way, but we're both over fifty and the truth is that I haven't been there for him. We haven't been there for each other. And I can't tell if we've failed or just been true to where life has taken us. I've learned, after all this way, that *brother* means *of the same source*. Strangely, it contains the word, *broth*, which means *made of the same thin soup*. And we are that. O we are that. I can taste the boil that has made us thin. I'm sorry, Howard. I'm not even sure for what. I carry you, my brother. Though I'm sure you bear the weight alone.

MOTHER AND CHILD
(IN BARCELONA)

Sitting in the square sipping water as two guitarists stroll among us. A young woman with a hard face approaches, a small child cradled on her hip. With emptiness in her eyes, she speaks in a language I don't understand, something other than Spanish. She points to her mouth, then the child. I have very little money left. She senses my confusion and points to my bottle of water, half-full, then points to her child again. She seems rather well-dressed to be begging, but I can never know all the costumes grief comes in. So I give her my water. She backs into the crowd. I close my eyes and listen to the sad guitarists. When I open them, I see the young mother meet up with another. They compare what they've managed. Then, the one who came to me begins to swagger, bites the cap from the water bottle, and swigs it down, offering none to her child. They laugh. She tosses the empty bottle in the narrow street and they vanish. Does this make my small offering any less? Any more? What if she were truly starving, she and her child? Would my half bottle have really mattered? It takes so much and so little to reach out to another. The guitarists break into song, as if to say giving quenches its own thirst.

BURNING THE WRAPPER

The first of me, so eager to be great,
to set things ablaze, shunned everything
ordinary. I hunted the burn of a champion's
hip. I yearned for the havoc great music
can play on the soul. But truth, regarded
as a prize, is as lonely as it is magnificent.
Thrones only have room for one.

A little further on, the second of me
wanted to be covered by waves, to inhale
the stars, to think like a hawk and pluck
truth from the fields. I so wanted to be a
special messenger of grace. But it was
not enough to alter what I sensed
about the hidden order of things.

Soon, my ego began to tire and the
third of me had a dark, soft belly. I let
others draw close. I asked more questions,
not really interested in answers, but more
in the face below the face about to speak.

Then, after chasing God's light for thirty
years, I fell ill and all I had assumed was up
for grabs. And in that falling, this odd reflection—
bent and distorted in the hospital chrome
as late sun flooded my pillow.

I was dead in the chrome, alive on the pillow,
a quiet breath between—dead, alive—at once.
Finally, I understood the breath between.

In every reflection since—in the car hood
waxed, in the florist's window out from under
its cloud, in the soft eye of my partner stripped
of worry—there waits our life, our death.

Oddly, it does not scare. For now,
I feel the quiet breath, and the place to which
I transcend now is here. And while there still exists
this veil about the world which must be burned till
what is left is real, the life—ain't it a kick—has
burned the veil that was me.

THE MYSTERY OF ILLNESS

It is said out of emptiness we can create dis-ease
and even if that dis-ease grew into a world
the way the earth grew out of God's emptiness,
we are not Gods and cannot bear it. It replaces us,
until severely empty we must fill ourselves endlessly
or comply like a secret to bareness.

It is said that those who are ill understand
the beauty of erosion and the power of falling water,
and those who are cut by simply living face two forms
of dis-ease: one from the friction of living and one
from not accepting what is.

It is said that those in pain can no longer fear pain
the way those in water can no longer stay dry.
And just as one who soothes another's loneliness
is made less lonely, those who accept another's
pain are made more whole.

It is said that those who have been empty and ill
know these are mysterious seasons. And those still
wet with pain know, be it physicians or lovers,
they cannot be cured by anyone whose
emptiness is greater than their own.

I have been all these emptinesses
and still, I am alive. What better proof
a pebble can sing.

CARRIED HOME

There comes a time
when there is nothing to say.

Like a bird who unexpectedly
launches into open space
a thousand feet up, the heart
after laboring is stunned
to find itself in such vastness.

After so many bruises,
the tongue rests like a feather
approaching its own image
on a lake.

GOD'S TIMING

When the lip is cut, no matter how,
the need to heal makes us chew
slower, and drink to one side. It makes
us speak only when we have something
to say. These are not bad things.

When the mind is cut, by a truth
too sharp to hold, it makes us bleed
the things we cling to. If lucky, we
bleed the things that no longer work.

When the self others have sealed us in
is cut, it lets us escape with only
what we were given at birth.

While there are terrible ways to be
opened, there is no such thing as a bad
opening. It's all about God's timing.
Not open enough and we fester. Open
too long and we become a wound.

If you speed up how a flower blooms,
it appears to be escaping. If you slow
down the way a crisis explodes what we
know, it appears we are transforming.

Hard as it is to embrace, crises are
flowers opening what we refuse
to open by ourselves.

Crossing Over

If you can't cross over alive,
how can you cross when you're dead?

— Kabir

THE LEAVING

When I told them I was leaving, one stared a long
time. Another muttered, "I always knew you would."
The cold one added, "Do you have any salt?"
But the one who loved me said, "I know
you must go" and took my hand.

When I asked them to come along,
the one who stared cried, and the mutterer
grew angry, "You know I'm not free that way."
While the one looking for salt pretended not to hear.
But the one who loved me smiled, "I will be there
before you open your eyes."

I couldn't explain my going, just
that my soul was now a flower
with a thirst for simple light.

FOR CRYING OUTLOUD

Always, afraid to let out a cry,
to make a noise, like those Jews
waiting in line at Baba Yar,
holding still when hit, showing nothing.
Mother seethed, erupted, smoldered.
I absorbed, threw my attention
on her like water. But it was
never enough. There was always
more fire than I had water.
And even when leaving home,
I looked for fires to put out,
thought this was love.
Now I am tired of chasing
a storm that has run out of land.
Let mother burn wherever I have
found her, put her, feared her.
Let her burn up. It is all she ever
wanted: not to light or to warm,
just to burn.

Now let what I feel be heard.
Like wind through trees.
Like love through hurt.
Let me throw water on myself.
Let the cries rise like steam.

MORE MYSTERIOUS THAN REGRET

It seems whenever I'm in San Francisco, I think of them. This time, it's the smell of bacon that pulls me back. Dad was always up first. Mom, letting slices curl in the pan. He, already in the basement sanding some piece of wood into a finer version of what he dreamt but couldn't speak. The bacon grease on my fingers pulls me to them. To his stroke when he clung to me like a frightened child. The sweet gristle pulls me through the long cloud of all we've done to each other. We haven't talked in nine years. Hard as that's been, I've been able to heal. I feel guilty saying this. What were the good things? There had to be good things. Why are they so slippery? The gristle sticks. I am 55. He is 86. There is much I would undo, but this is about something more mysterious than regret. It doesn't really matter what transpired, so significant to us. It was nothing extraordinary in the history of fathers and sons. What seems unbreachable is the step he won't take to find me, though he knows where I am.

Here, by the Bay, I feel the lap of the water and think of the sailboat he made which took us where the wind shut us all up. I have begun to mourn them. Like his wooden boat, I've made a new home of myself. And just last week, I discovered in some old letters that when his father had a heart attack, before I was born, Dad took Mom and went to Florida, then drove to Yosemite on an adventure that kept them from looking back. They were young. It was their chance. His father never really recovered. He was ill for years and, though they returned, my father was never really there for him. My grandfather died when I was two. I look more like him the older I get. Now I'm in awe that by doing what I've needed to do, to find myself and live with myself—to seize my chance—I have been an instrument in my father's karma. Now he will probably die without his son, as his father did.

How is this possible? I have earned my choices by which to live. Just how does that lead him to where he was born to go? I don't know what shaped him. I can barely understand what has shaped me. And what did his father do or not do to him?

All the deep banter by philosophers about destiny and free will; only to see, while eating bacon by the San Francisco Bay, that they are the same. One is the instrument of the other. And just as evolution and erosion are God's tools for this ongoing creation, I'm coming to see how serving as obstacles for each other is part of God's friction that sparks our little fires by which we might eventually see.

Sadly, beautifully, we have arrived exactly where we have chosen and are meant to be. I realize now how my mother resented me for believing in a life she'd lost faith in. I can taste her slapping me when I was fifteen, for not doing her bidding and for being what she couldn't find in herself. I saw the anger in her eyes and how much she meant for it to hurt. I realized then how they both chose anger as their antenna in the world. It was just a slap on a weekday after school in my room, but that slap set a story in motion that has led to tragedy and liberation, to love of self and world and God. As the one inch that doesn't freeze in the arctic night eventually causes a flood in Indonesia, these minute slaps in the region of human coldness flood our lives in the years to come.

But before all that, I would wake to the smell of bacon on Saturday mornings, eager to feel the press of her apron. I'd sit in awe on the top step, while the world cooked, watching my father carve some new piece of the Ark that would save us all.

LESSON FROM THE FARTHER SHORE

We had rowed past all signs of human life
and simply waited, drifting in the water, not
really sure what we were waiting for, and then,
the clearness of the water enlarged and the lily
pad wavered, its red underside growing redder
for the sun on its back, and high above us, two
enormous birds: gliding, soaring, wings out-
stretched, way above the trees. They were
too large for hawk, too thick-chested for heron,
their entire length black, too massive for crow.
They began to ride the currents and we kept still
and they didn't pump their massive wings once.
We watched them glide above the entangled forest
beyond our need to name them, and one came
lower, the sun making its spread body a jet-black
silhouette. I realized in that moment that this
is what I hope for: to find the unseeable current
above the entanglement of things and soar
without effort until work and play are one.

The two soared for so long that we were forced
to let go of them as a wonderful snapshot
that had opened our day. No, we were now a part
of their day. Never had I seen anything so still
and so in motion at the same time.

Now I understand: this is the majesty of flight.
And the majesty of love, of friendship,
they shouted to us wordlessly, is to ride our
separate currents wherever they take us,
never losing sight of each other, until

like these unnameable birds,
wing is indistinct from current
and self is indistinct from God.

YOU'RE LOOKING GREAT

Everyone is interested,
intrigued with how I made
the tumor shrink. How I
conquered this and
conquered that.

But how do lowlands
conquer floods?

Everyone
with a weak heart
wants me to say
it was my mind.

But the mind's
a trojan horse.

It's larger than
medicine and poetry
combined.

And just last night, a
bright tigress of a woman
read my silence as
a triumph of will.

I watched God's light
braid in her hair.

HOW I LOVED THEM

Like boats untied set next to each other in the ocean.
When the storm cleared, we couldn't find each other.

For the fourth time since losing them, the weeping cherry is blooming across the street. It showers into blossom for three days in May. I stand beneath it and marvel at how such thin flowers appear out of wood. They sway over me with branches of pink little chimes so delicate I have to stop every thought of pain in order to hear them. Less covers me than in the previous life. I feel more and hurt more. But know more of joy. I miss them terribly. The cherry weeps. I stand like a stump, puddles draining around me. All this to say, I have lost the oldest of friends.

Where are their hands? John, Lin, Cindy, Diane, Alan, Nur, Fitz, Wally, Ed, even Ann? Where the deep impressions of loving them for the first time? Where is John's barn-sized laugh? Or Alan's sad guitar?

I wouldn't be here without them. They held me while the tumors grew and ran warm water on my swollen head. One propped me up while another fed me sips of tomorrow. But when I left Ann, they shunned me and a messy, darker story began. Like the crazed mariner, I can't finish the story. Did they really need to cut me off? There are so many things splintered between us. They misled me because they felt misled. One drew me close then slapped me down. I pushed off others in order to get free. We all scrambled into old positions. But not old enough. Now they feel like roots ripped from the heart.

Now, my ripped heart lives in another country and we don't seem to understand each other anymore. Though I still feel indentured to the past. I was saying so to yet another stranger the other day when she held me up, put her hand on my chest, and offered, "As brave as they were, it's harder to stand by those who live." I know she is right. I know we lose nothing and everything. Yet this is not about loss, but the mystery of how a path of flight becomes invisible once flown; how the path of love once lived is there but not—always present but not presentable.

Now I stand beneath the weeping cherry, a sorry bird whose song is his nest. And there is this cloud that comes and goes whenever I sing which makes me sad, which holds me under like some dark hand pushing my face into the crack in my heart, saying, *Look, look, look what you've done.*

Wally is dead, his glasses on his desk. Alan is enraged, his guitar in the corner, his eyes on fire. My parents are so far into their smallness that no known language works. John won't answer my calls. And my divorce to Ann is final. All because I've dropped my secret ways.

At first, I was distracted by the pain into understanding it, into righting it, into making sure my side was known, but the hurt keeps falling inside like a knife in a well. I keep waiting for it to land, but late last night, a voice in dream said, "Open like a canyon and all your noise will disappear." O lone cloud above the mountain, what did you give up to become so light?

I am becoming at once particular and cosmic, no in between. The names I've been given, the shames I've earned, the dreams I haven't been able to realize—all are burning away. I am all right and not all right, at one and in pieces. More in love than ever and more alone. I cannot make sense of these shifts. But then I'm not really trying, for if I've learned one thing after all this way, it's that the creatures who live beneath all sense are the ones who know grace—the owl, the eagle, the angelfish, the golden retriever eager for his master to return.

How many times has something dear fallen out from under till, like so many before me, I find myself bent, uttering, "So this is the beginning." Like Ghalib from Persia, I realize that "All is one footprint." Broken open like Dōgen in a northern province of Japan, "I hear the one true thing." With the German Hölderlin, I finally admit, "We waste our life waiting, and I haven't the faintest idea how to act or talk." And from my knees with

Augustine, there is nothing left but to confess, "I came to love you too late. What did I know? You were inside me." So this is the beginning, unraveling like an empty basket till what carries and what is carried are the same.

THE DREAM OF HEALING

I rest in a circle of those still here, all of
us humbled, each taking a turn telling
the story of what has fallen away.

A woman in her thirties is speaking
of her cancer. I wince to hear of the
intravenous treatments. But suddenly,
she says it was those who came before
who were pumped into our veins.
It was this that saved us.

Somehow, I know who these spirits
are. I see their faces. They are people I
have loved, some no longer here: Nur,
John, Grandma, Jane. I start to weep
to think they're in our veins.

Our weeping turns the needles into
laurel leaves. She sprinkles them
on our faces.

MADE LESS AND MORE

Several are gone now.
I could tell their stories,
but not here. Just know
that one was a flame
calmed into a flower.
Another a turtle
broken into a deer.
And the insecure one
who loved like a wave.
And the stubborn one
who entered water
like a stone.

But more today,
there is something
about being made less
and continuing
that inexplicably
makes the
journey
holy.

Still, each time
someone dies,
I become a statue
whose eyes
freeze over,
whose heart
flakes away,
leaving a hole

for memories to
drift through.

And the feeling
of someone gone
moving through
so far inside
is an odd weight.

On early fall days,
like today, there is
nothing to hold on to,
and yet the wind
says, what else
do you need?

RELEASED

Today, my annual checkup and at the end,
Janet says, "Let me know if you want to be released."
I am stunned. She says, "It's been ten years. You no longer
have to come." We stare at each other. She smiles till Peggy,
who put the needles so carefully in my hardened arm, pops
in to hug me, and Robert, who read Neruda while I was
sweating with fear, cries in the parking lot. And I come home
to Susan and we make love and, while gently inside her, I
scream in my pillow, feeling all the needles that prodded me
to stay here. Was Lazarus so poked and stunned? What
have my veins done with all the punctures? Do my hips
still hold the marrow-gouge? My heart like a torn tent
flaps, so glad to be flapping. My mind, a cut sail
that can barely hold the wind.

THE ACHE OF BEING ALIVE

It's with me now,
as I pour the coffee,
as I raise the blind,
as I pick up twigs
from the lawn.

I used to fear it,
try to hush it,
but it has been more loyal
than those I've loved.

It asks so little.

Only to sip
where I am softest
and then like a babe
it goes to sleep.

When in its company
I want for nothing.

DROPPING BELOW

I have a friend, Daniel, who is a widower after eighteen years of marriage. It's been four years since his dear wife, Rachel, died and he has nosed through the waters of his grief like a widowed whale, sending out his heart-breaking whine, almost inaudible because it's underwater, as he searches the world for her, though we all hold him close and tell him that she's gone. That he needs others is a blessing. His grief has been a teacher for us all.

Just last month, we were up late, sipping our fourth coffee around a table she used to sit at, and he uttered while staring at his spoon, "I still feel her everywhere and can't find her anywhere." I am in awe of his love. Privately, we all have our own arguments about him which carry their charge, as we all fear being him. The essence of these arguments rests between feeling that he needs to move on and the acceptance that this is how he is moving on.

The other night, when he went to the bathroom, the same argument erupted, which he overheard, and he came back to the table, his hands gripping the air, "Don't you think I know I am stuck?" He paced around, "But we loved each other for eighteen years. She knew me better than anyone on earth. And I her." He stalled near the window, "I've lost my best friend . . ."

Then Roy, the one most troubled that Daniel can't move on, blurted out, "You don't want to move on, do you?" And Daniel began to weep, "That's the heart of it . . . I don't . . . because I know that once I love another, Rachel will disappear forever . . . Don't you think I want to love again, to feel that place inside come alive?"

We fell silent. This was the crux of it. He was stretched on his own cross of keeping his love for Rachel alive, and his need to love again in order to keep living. He was stuck between lives. As if he heard our thoughts, he said,

"More painful now than her death is the prospect of letting her go and watching her recede into the very air . . . I don't know how to do that."

I could tell that all this scared Roy and that he would stop coming around. And I could tell that I loved Daniel all the more for his courage in letting his love of Rachel and his love of life wrestle within his broken heart. Then Daniel fell into his chair, more than sitting in it. I poured him another cup of coffee. It grew late. Roy went home and I rubbed Daniel's back. I could see in his eyes that he was rehearsing, could almost hear his whale-like thoughts whispering, "Forgive me, my love, I have to live . . . "

AS MOONLIGHT
(FOR ANN)

When we began, everything held wonder
in a secret place that was shouting
like a waterfall.

I can't tell the whole story here
except to say that thirty years have passed
and we have been friends, lovers, have
saved each other's lives, been ex-lovers,
difficult friends, have felt discounted
and betrayed, have almost walked away,
have gasped onto the shore of forgiveness,
have found love in other eyes, and harshly
and sweetly, we have been worn
free of all names. We don't know
what to call each other.

Now, states away,
you are losing your sight
and I am creaky in the knees.

And I have cried in the midst of telling
what can't be told, sitting before strangers,
catching myself saying, "I found her injecting
a syringe in an orange. When I asked,
she said she was practicing how to
keep me from getting nauseous."

No way to sum up thirty years.
Or being pulled back into life. Or
being forced to bow to the changes

wrought by God's fugitive, time.

How do we talk to anyone about
what was held and dropped and lost
and still is always there? I swear I feel
eight and eighty at once. And you?
I pray you are well loved.

We are fallen limbs drifting apart
on the lake of nights, except as
moonlight paints our lives.

NOTHING HAS GROWN OVER

Something very close to the skin
has burned off, rubbed sheer by the
closeness of death.

Now, I go to parties with
nothing on but skin, where nice young
women tell me how they've evened off their
lives, to guard against the lows, how
they've matted down the joys.

I tell this one a dream, of "a hairless
man dancing through a tumorous field
and when he stops, he starts
to sink into the earth."

She wants to go for another drink.
I grab her arm, lightly. She politely
excuses herself. The words fume
about my lips.

You see. Something very safe
has burned away. But it's making me
stronger. And simple tasks are
magnetic and bare.

Like bailing the old dory at the lake,
scooping the cool syrup of the earth
back into the earth, bucket after
bucket, loving it more
than pain, scooping what
has seeped in from the deep,

watching our ribs swell,
then pouring it back
so we can drift on.

FOUR DREAMS OF DEATH

At first I was at a party with people I barely knew. I was nursing a drink, thinking about leaving, when a tall slender figure approached in a black hooded robe holding a mask. He was very annoying. He circled me, kept poking his skeletal mask in my face. When I turned to confront him, I realized it was Michael, an old friend who couldn't face my illness and who never called or even sent a card.

Michael was drunk, masquerading as death. Someone to my left said, "By your looks, he must be important to you." I smirked, "He's insignificant." Someone else, a woman I think, spun into the conversation, "Why insignificant?" I said, "Because friendship which fails when put to the test is insignificant." Michael was in and out of my face. I waved him off, as I would a mosquito. The man to my left, a gentle man with an enormous grin, said, "But aren't you capable of that? Aren't we all?" I shot back, "He didn't even try!"

At this, Michael muttered something behind his mask and the woman said, "He's saying he's sorry." But the gentle man said, "No, he's saying he isn't Michael." The man leaned closer to better understand. Michael muttered almost painfully. The gentle man remarked flatly, "He says he's the ugly side of you."

I hated Michael for doing that and left, but as I crossed the doorway I was falling into a very deep space, beyond any sense of gravity, beyond any sense of direction, and coming at me, again, was a skeleton in a hood, this time its sockets blood red. This was no failed friend wearing a mask. I was falling into the dark field of my own death.

Shocked, I backed away, as much as one can in a weightless sea of black. It kept lunging. Finally, I was so angry, I screamed but the scream was underwater or, rather, under life. It kept lunging my way. I waved my arms as if treading the weightless black and thought with force, *I Refuse to let you land. Refuse.* It kept lunging. I kept treading with all my strength and felt exhausted in a slow-motion dance which, only while sustained, kept the bones of death at bay. This went on for what seemed like hours. I was losing consciousness, losing strength in my arms, but the dance kept using me now, the way a storm uses a torn piece of roof to announce its power. I nodded off repeatedly and with each inhalation the bones came so close I felt the aura of their heat. As I tried to get a look, the bones of death kissed my neck, burning a hole in my skin. I winced and reeled, falling backwards in the blackness and, as if the psychic figure were a part of me, it reeled in the opposite direction, as if a mirror image, its bone lips smoking as I passed out.

When I came to, I thought I was in a sunlit grove, but I was still in the dream. Everything was quiet and safe. Every leaf and pine needle caught the light so delicately, making me want to touch them all. As the sun moved through the quiet forest, it lit a small stone which I picked up. It felt warm. I couldn't quite remember where I'd been, not in all this light. I knelt in the leaves which were wet and my knees began to soak and I began to cry for all the things I've had to let go of. I put the stone aside and ran my hands through the leaves and felt a piece of wood, perhaps a fallen branch. I brushed the leaves from it and, as I picked it up, it turned into a snake which, though I dropped it, kept rising till its head spread into the dark hood with the skeletal face. Terrified, I fell back. It held itself aloft, hovering before me. The light avoided it. I said, "Why won't you leave me alone?" It said, "O, I haven't come for you. You survived." "Then what? What?!" "Just for the things you love."

I moved into the light. It hovered in the dark, "And this is how it will happen. You'll overturn a stone or twig or piece of conversation with a friend—and I'll be there—" "Will you always terrify me?" It started to sink back into the earth, "That's up to you." Again, it seemed a piece of fallen branch, "I am just here." The wind covered the branch with leaves, "Just here."

I stood there for the longest time, unsure if this was yet a dream within a dream or was I, in fact, awake. I began to walk the woods, thinking of the things I've watched die, from birds on asphalt to lambs in winter brooks to fish rolled on the beach to mythic grandmothers on foreign continents. I walked and walked. The forest seemed endless and in the light I felt as if my body couldn't contain me, but in the shade I thought my body would come in on me and crush my very mind. At last, I tried to step only in the pockets of light and then I found a path, worn but not recently used, and so I took it.

Off in the distance, a figure was walking toward me, as if in my cadence, stopping when I'd stop, shuffling when I'd shuffle, pacing faster when I'd step it up. When close enough to make it out, it seemed a sage with a flowing beard. Then closer still, my broken grandmother while she could still walk. Then, the me I'd always hoped to be. Then, all at once, standing tall, my father without his scowl. That made me greet it with a burst. Upon it squarely, it was the damn hooded skeleton.

I was so fed up, enraged, that I raised both fists and began to pound its featureless face. It was burning my hands, but I pounded till the face bones cracked. I pounded, making the gutteral noises of a spirit tired of being in a human body, and then it shattered, only to re-form into two skeletal heads. I was aghast. For the briefest instant, they looked at each other and seemed my parents. I rushed them both.

To my amazement, they turned into the reddest flower with bright, moist petals. Everything turned calm, and the flower beneath death began like a backwards film to return to its seed, then to its previous blossom, then to its previous seed, over and over, toward the beginning. I knelt before it in awe, "How could I have known?"

It kept blossoming backwards in the most beautiful display of softness I have ever seen and seemed to speak, not in words, though I heard it as words, "I will appear to you however you want." I thought, *I don't understand.* It kept undoing its marvelous blossoms, "I will take on the affects you fear or the stillness you dream of." I thought quietly, *I want to stay here.*

It offered, "You can." Then with a burst of color, "But you will always have to break through."

I thought painfully, *But what of the ache?* It radiated its softness, "Don't you realize yet?" I felt like a petal unfolding. It unwrapped me, "The more you want to live, the more you will hurt." I went to ask why, but in the unfolding of the flower beneath death, I could find no such word.

SURVIVING HAS MADE ME CRAZY

I eat flowers now and birds follow me.
I open myself like an inlet
and dolphin energies
swim on through.

Wherever I go, I remain silent
and the silence begins to glow
till one eye in the light
outsees two in the dark.

When asked, I now hesitate
for there are so many ways
to love the earth.

I water things now constantly:
water the hearts of dead friends with light,
the sores of the living with anything warm,
water the skies with a thousand affections
and follow the voices of animals
into grasses that move like ocean.

I eat flowers now and birds come.
I eat care and things to love arrive.
I eat time and as I age
whatever I swallow grows timeless.

I eat and undie
and water my doubts
with silence
and birds come.

Gratitudes

In a way, you could say that everything I've ever written has been an attempt at gratitude. I am 55. So, in a book like this, gratitude peels all the way back to birth. Still, it helps to be clear what I am grateful for. Quite simply and profoundly, for the kindness and courage of so many, often unseen, who have allowed me to live, the way quiet hands lift a baby turtle to the side of the road. Because I have been spared, I know how very much we need each other, how very much we need the earth and the stars. How very much they need us. How much we need the children who carry the mystery before life interferes, and how it all goes on whether we answer this need or not. There are too many names to list, too many words which will miss anyway. You can't see it but I am bowing to you, to life, to the fact that we will do what we need to live. We will sift what others discard and find a way to tomorrow. It is a brutal miracle for which I am sweetly grateful.

*A special gratitude to Peter Cusack, a former student and fellow artist. CavanKerry brought us back together after twenty years. To Peter who kindly lent his gifts in creating the original painting that serves as the cover . . . how fitting that the teacher should become the student . . .